HOW TO: WRITE BETTER COPY

Steve Harrison was European Creative Director (Ogilvy-One) and Global Creative Director (Wunderman) either side of starting his own agency, HTW. At HTW, he won more Cannes Lions in his discipline than any creative director in the world. That discipline was direct marketing, which means his copy was judged not by how clever it was but by how many things it sold. When he left agency life, *Campaign* magazine described him as 'the greatest direct marketing creative of his generation'. Steve's work appears in *The D&AD Copy Book*, which features the world's top 50 copywriters of the past 50 years. His *How to Do Better Creative Work* became the most expensive advertising book of all time when it traded on Amazon.co.uk at £3,854 a copy. It is published in English, Mandarin, Spanish and Italian.

how to: ACADEMY launched in September 2013. Since then it has organized over 400 talks and seminars on Business, Lifestyle, and Science & Technology, which have been attended by 40,000 people. The aim of the series is to anticipate the needs of the reader by providing clarity, precision and know-how in an increasingly complex world.

STEVE HARRISON

HOW TO: WRITE BETTER COPY

bluebird
books for life

First published 2016 by Bluebird
an imprint of Pan Macmillan
20 New Wharf Road, London N1 9RR
Associated companies throughout the world
www.panmacmillan.com

ISBN 978-1-5098-1457-2

Copyright © How To Academy Limited 2016

9 8 7 6 5 4 3 2 1

A CIP catalogue record for this book is available from the British Library.

Printed and bound by CPI Group (UK) Ltd, Croydon, CR0 4YY

Visit **www.panmacmillan.com** to read more about all our books
and to buy them. You will also find features, author interviews and
news of any author events, and you can sign up for e-newsletters
so that you're always first to hear about our new releases.

For Mo and Ol

Contents

1:

WHAT YOU REALLY WANT IS 'EFFECTIVE' COPY

This book's title refers to writing 'better' copy. And, as we'll see, one of the ways you achieve this is by choosing your words carefully.

You should keep asking yourself, 'Does this word really convey what I mean?'

For example, I'm looking at the title right now and I think it could be more accurate. Because what I really hope to show you is how to write effective copy. And by 'effective' I mean copy that does three things:

It gets your readers to notice it.

It gets them to engage with it.

And it gets them to do what you want them to do.

Let's start with getting noticed

If you're writing marketing copy, spare a thought for your reader. She's bombarded by thousands of commercial messages every day. And, on the morning you send her yours, the poor girl will have been subjected to another onslaught.

Years ago, I nearly cut short my fledgling copywriting career when I saw some daunting Nielsen research. It said the average UK citizen was exposed to 2,200 marketing salvoes every day. Worse still, it showed that twenty-four hours later, only eight had hit their target.

Since then, our industry has invented new weapons of mass distraction. All are aimed at catching the reader's eye, yet none have been any more successful than the equivalent of the longbow and catapult that I used when I started as a writer.

According to our industry's wisest blogger, Bob Hoffman, consumer interaction with this online advertising is essentially non-existent. For example, the average click rate for banner ads is eight in 10,000, and consumer engagement with Twitter posts is around three in 10,000.[1]

Why the failure? Well, the people you're aiming at have a shield that protects them from the shell-shock that would otherwise result from this non-stop barrage. It's a formidable defence-mechanism, but it *is* possible to get through.

Here's an example of one that made it – and one that didn't.

From 1960 to some time in the noughties, Volkswagen positioned itself as the most reliable car in the world. In the UK this was summed up in the strapline: 'If only everything in life was as reliable as a Volkswagen.'

If you are over forty years old, then you'll have been exposed to this line. There's also a good chance you'll remember it. Why? Because reliability is an interesting quality in a car, especially when it comes to buying or selling it second-hand. And, as a result, VW's promise may well have made it through your defences.

However, in 2007, the Direktors at VW decided they needed something different, and between then and last December, every piece of VW marketing in the world carried a new strapline.

You were exposed to the line for over eight years. However, the fact that you saw it thousands of times does not mean you noticed it.

VW had certainly been firing blanks at the twenty-two people who attended a seminar I gave last week. When I asked if anyone in the audience could tell me the VW strapline, there were lots of quizzical faces, then a tentative hand went up and its owner muttered: 'Ermm, "Vorsprung durch Technik"?'

Which suggests that VW's efforts to pierce the carapace of consumer indifference succeeded only in reminding some people of the slogan that has graced Audi's advertising for the past thirty-four years.

As the VW example indicates, getting ignored is easy. Getting noticed is much harder, but it is possible.

A recent YouGov poll showed that 'consumers respond well to good advertising that is relevant to them. When advertising is done right and is interesting, informative and relevant it is still the best way for brands to communicate with customers.'[2]

Jakob Nielsen offers the same encouragement in 'Legibility, Readability, and Comprehension: Making Users Read Your Words': 'On the average web page visit, users read only 28% of the words.' But he adds that users 'do read web content, particularly when it includes information of interest to them.' As the leading authority on how to write for the web, Nielsen's advice is worth following.[3]

We'll talk later about being interesting, and informative and relevant. But let's move on to the next step:

Getting your reader to engage with your copy

If you've got them to notice your message, well done. But really, that's just the start.

Because at this stage they are only willing to skim your copy rather than read it. And in skimming, they're subconsciously working out the risk and reward of a) wasting their time by reading on, or b) finding out something interesting or useful.

If you're writing for a website then it isn't just your reader who is judging you. Google's people could be rating your copy right now. And if they think it is difficult to get into, dull and badly written, you'll be punished with a drop in the search ranking and a fall in traffic.

There are several ways to win over both Google and your reader: the words you use, the order you put them in, and the way you lay them out. All of which we will discuss later.

But bear this in mind: even when your reader has opted to read on, that decision can be changed in the blink of an eye. Actually, it happens faster than that. Our eyes fix on the screen for just 250 milliseconds before jumping on another seven to nine letters. Then they fix for another 250 milliseconds before jumping on again, or giving up completely.

So, you cannot relax. You've never 'got them hooked'. If the reader momentarily gives you the benefit of the doubt you must strive to keep their attention for another 250 milliseconds . . . and another . . . and another . . . and another . . . until your message is delivered.

In other words, you must get them to engage with your copy.

Now there's a lot of talk in marketing circles about

'engagement', but not much in the way of definition. So here's one for you: readers become engaged with what you have written when they can see themselves in the story you are telling.

Take it from me, this definition applies to any writing, be it the kind of commercial copy that you are working on or a piece of bestselling fiction.

Actually, don't take it from me – take it from the chap who knows more about shifting shelf-loads of bestselling fiction than anyone else on this planet.

Stephen King is sure that 'book buyers aren't attracted, by and large, by the literary merits of a novel; book buyers want a good story to take with them on the airplane, something that will fascinate them, then pull them in and keep them turning pages. This happens, I think, when people recognize the people in a book, their behaviours, their surroundings and their talk. When the reader hears strong echoes of his or her own life and beliefs, he or she is apt to become more invested in the story.'[4]

Only when this happens will you get them to resist the urge to seek more interesting alternatives (such as the articles that surround your ad) or easier options (such as not reading anything at all).

And if you can pull that off, then you're ready to achieve your final goal:

Getting your reader to do what you want them to do

Getting readers to engage with your copy is so difficult, many marketers see it as an end in itself.

Indeed, according to the Fournaise Marketing Group, which specializes in measuring marketing performance, most marketers 'are mistaking engagement for conversion by measuring key performance indicators such as website traffic, video views and open rates, rather than sales.'[5]

Getting people reading but not buying is like packing your bar with Muslims and Methodists. And Jerome Fournaise, Fournaise's Global CEO, concludes that marketers who act this way 'need to stop living in their la-la land and start behaving like real business people'.[6]

If you don't want offices in la-la land, you need to accept that your copy is an exercise in competitive persuasion. Moreover, you're using the written word to manipulate your readers. Very often, your aim is to change a course of action they've already decided upon, and get them to follow your suggested route.

It could be you want them to take the ten quid they give to the Save the Children Fund every quarter, and text it to Friends of the Earth instead.

Or free up the £30,000 they've got tucked away in the building society and invest it in one of your equity funds.

Or maybe you want your client to rethink their decision to divert 60 per cent of their marketing budget into this season's fashionable medium.

Or you'd like your boss to review the way she's divvied up the company's wages budget, and top your salary up with the extra £3,000 that you think you deserve.

Like I said, it's manipulation. And it is very difficult for two reasons.

Why it's difficult

Firstly, in many cases you'll be trying to get someone to literally 'change their mind'. And that brings you head-to-head with something psychologists call 'confirmation bias', or your reader's unwillingness to accept things that run counter to their point of view.

It's hard to overcome this because, according to Michael Frank, a neuroscientist at Brown University, 'This bias has a physical basis in the neurotransmitter dopamine, which acts as a reward signal to the brain. Acting on the prefrontal cortex, it inclines us to ignore evidence that challenges long-held views, keeping us from having to constantly revise the mental shorthand we use to understand the world.'[7]

Or, as my dear old mum says, 'we're set in our ways'.

The second reason lies in the sheer difficulty of getting the reader to understand what you mean.

To get your message, the reader has to decipher the squiggles you've put on the page or the screen. There's nothing innate about this. It comes as naturally to us as knowing how to play the banjo or speak Latin.

As Maryanne Wolf explains in her book *Proust and the Squid*, 'we were never born to read. Human beings invented reading only a few thousand years ago. And with this invention, we rearranged the very organization of our brain.'

Such improvisation is difficult because this primate's brain of ours evolved to hunt and gather on the African savannah – not to scan copy on a PC screen. So we writers must make it as easy as possible for the reader's old grey matter to work out what our squiggles mean.

Making it easy for your reader

When it comes to making it easy, my twenty-five years as a copywriter have led me to believe that the brain prefers signposts (headlines and subheads) that tell it what's coming; squiggles (words) it immediately recognizes; and combinations of squiggles (sentences and paragraphs) that are structured in a way that aids understanding.

I'm delighted to say that my hunches are borne out by the research of psycholinguists, neuroscientists and cognitive and behavioural psychologists who have studied the reader's brain. In fact, Yellowlees Douglas has written an excellent book with that very title, and we'll be making regular visits to its pages.

But choosing the right words and setting them out in the correct order is only part of the battle. For if your reader isn't interested in the subject of your copy, it doesn't matter how adept you are at putting the squiggles together.

So how do you achieve the most difficult task: coming up with something that the reader wants to read? How will your message stand out from the thousands of marketing communications that appear that day?

And, more to the point, how can it compete against the Facebook posts, forums and football results; the traffic updates, tweets and TV shows; and the pub chat, podcasts and quick sessions on *League of Legends* that are vying for your prospect's attention?

Let's see, shall we?

2:

THE THINKING BEFORE THE WRITING

The best creative work produced by London's advertising industry is delivered every Friday at 5.00 p.m.

People cheer. Corks pop. And the person who takes delivery often keeps it for the rest of their working lives.

The creative I'm talking about here is the leaving card that's given to the colleague whose last day at the agency is coming to a close.

And it is brilliant because the team who did it know all about its recipient's likes and dislikes, fears and foibles – and what they spend most afternoons looking at when they should be working.

Creative ideas feed on such familiarity. And if you are to write something the reader will find so interesting they'll want to keep it then you, too, will need to know a lot about your subject.

Know your prospect . . .

Start by studying the data – both big and small. Better still, talk to your prospects and customers.

However, be wary of face-to-face interviews. As Swarthmore College professor of psychology Barry Schwartz tells us, people can be divided into 'satificers' and 'maximizers'. The former are happy with products and services that meet most of their needs in a satisfactory way. The latter agonize over the choice until the very best option comes along.[1]

Most people are satificers most of the time. However, they are occasional maximizers when it comes to important things such as choosing the place where they'll spend their precious two-week annual holiday, or the bar where they'll meet that person they really fancy.

The other occasion they become maximizers is when they are confronted by someone doing qualitative research. Then, regardless of whether the product in question is a sports car or a Mars bar, they become the most exacting of consumers.

For a more valid view of what people want and what they think, check the ratings, reviews and online forums where users swap news and advice about how a product works, and how well.

You'll get a similar insight by listening to customers at your call centre. Likewise, talk to the people who field comments on your Twitter feed. For many companies nowadays, Twitter's main commercial role is that of the canary in the coalmine – their customers' tweets being the first warning of dangerous dissatisfaction. Find out what they are saying.

And don't forget the folks who sell to customers all the time: your sales team. Spend time with them and learn the tricks of their trade.

. . . and your product

Once you know your prospect, move on to the product or service. Bob Levenson, who was the best copywriter at Doyle Dane Bernbach when it was the best creative shop in the world, explains why this is important: 'In order to be informative – never mind persuasive – you need to know how the car is put together, how the chicken is taken apart, what the surfactant does, what to expect in the foreign country, in what way is the oil "refined", etc. etc. In the absence of such knowledge you will be doomed to rely more and more on adjectives; always a mistake.'[2]

But where do you get this information? Well, here's how another great from that golden age of copywriting, Alfredo Marcantonio, goes about it: 'There are your notes from the factory visit. (You don't take notes? Well, body copy is a good reason to start.) Next, search the client's old ads for anything interesting or persuasive. And the competition's. (The most awful ads can harbour the most interesting facts.) After that, read all the brochures, technical sheets, independent tests and press cuttings you can. Even the annual report can contain a few gems.'[3]

At this point, you may have unearthed some insights that look like 'gems'. But if you *are* going through the annual report, chances are those gems will be things that the client's board members, City analysts and shareholders like the look of. But they're probably of little interest to the person you're writing to.

So, how do you keep focused on what your reader wants to know?

Some wise words from Howard Gossage

I was guided in this by two of the greats of American advertising. The first was the maverick copywriter Howard Gossage.

Gossage was advertising's biggest critic, and railed against the way it talked down to its audience. He argued for, and invented a style of, interactive advertising that fostered a dialogue between advertiser and reader.

And he knew how to start the dialogue. As he said, 'People read what interests them, and sometimes it's an ad.'[4]

When I read this, I saw it as advice to do more than just compete with the other ads that were trying to attract my prospect's attention – Gossage was saying that my copy had to be more interesting than the things that surrounded it.

So if we're writing a press ad, it has to compete with the newspaper's features, editorial and news items. Likewise, if we're writing an e-zine headline, it has to be as interesting as the emails, websites, blogs and forums that your prospect has logged on for in the first place.

Now, you may despair because you feel the thing you're selling can never be that fascinating. If so, let me share the advice I got from another advertising great, John Caples.

How to make your copy interesting

John Caples was the head of copy at Batten, Barton, Durstine & Osborn (which is today's BBDO) for much of the second half of the twentieth century. During that time, he tracked the results of the press ads his agency produced. He concluded that in order to be successful, your headline has to have one (or a combination) of three qualities:

If the headline arouses curiosity, that's good because we are a curious species. If you're in doubt, just look at the popularity of BuzzFeed. Only an innate curiosity would explain why three million people want to see '22 Celebrity Cat Ladies and Dog Dads Who Will Melt Your Cold Dead Heart'.

BuzzFeed has become immensely popular because it combines curiosity with the second quality Caples identified as essential to a successful headline: the imparting of news.

In fact, Caples noted that we are suckers for such claims as 'new' and 'improved'. And that you should pop one or both of these words into a headline whenever you can.

Why? Because as a species we survived and evolved by being alert to the unexpected, and fascinated by the unfamiliar. If, for example, the tribe at the bottom of the hill discovered a fearsome critter called a sabre-toothed tiger, it made sense for us to check it out.

This is how the human brain worked back then. It was preoccupied with survival. It scanned the horizon, and when it saw something new, three questions sprang to mind: 'Will it eat me? Can I eat it? Can I perpetuate my line by bonking it?'

Nothing much has changed. As Martin Weigel explains in his masterful blog post 'The fracking of attention', we are built 'to focus our finite mental resources on new sights, sounds, thoughts and feelings and to filter out the rest . . . So essential to any species' survival is this arousal by and adaptation to novelty that infants less than a day old will stare at a new image for about forty-one seconds – and then tune out when repeated exposures render it familiar.'[5]

Once that image becomes part of the baby's nursery wallpaper, the child moves on in search of new stimuli.

And so, as we grow, our curiosity feeds itself. Indeed, according to Dimitrios Tsivrikos, consumer and business psychologist at University College London, 'Receiving novel information activates the brain's reward pathway, which leads to a continuous cycle in which we are compelled to seek out more and more information.'[6]

Which means our curiosity and the quest for novelty are addictive. And this need governs our behaviour, regardless of whether we're hunting in the Amazon Rainforest or on amazon.com.

In the latter case, we also make the logical, if subconscious, assumption that if the manufacturer has gone to the trouble of introducing a 'new' and 'improved' line, then it must be more efficacious and therefore better. And therefore worth buying. And why might it be worth buying?

Well, that brings us to the kind of headline that, according to John Caples, is the most effective of them all.

The third thing Caples told us about headlines: appeal to your reader's self-interest

Once again, the oldest, most primitive part of our brain is taking over, and the survival instinct is to the fore. As Caples said, the headlines that get most attention 'are the ones which appeal to the reader's self-interest, that is headlines based on reader benefits. They offer readers something they want – and can get from you.'[7]

Caples's conclusions changed my approach to writing copy. I hope he'll have the same effect on you.

Instead of thinking about how you can sell the product or service, or how to get the reader to buy into your idea, start by looking at it from their point of view. Think about what's in it for them. What need of theirs will it fill? What advantage will it give them?

These are the only parts of your message that'll really grab them. Write about anything else and your reader's apt to abandon your text in favour of some drying paint that needs watching.

Find their problem and your solution

To get and keep your reader's attention, start by asking yourself these two questions:

What is the problem they are facing at the moment?

What is the solution provided by the product or service that I am selling?

If you are writing an email pitching a client for work, a proposal to your colleagues, a think piece or anything that involves an idea you want people to adopt, just substitute 'idea' for 'product or service'.

Whatever it is, if you cannot answer those two key questions, there's no point in writing anything. The reader will not notice your headline, subject line or strapline because there'll be nothing in there for them.

So keep searching.

Here's an example that did well in the Press Category at the Cannes Lions Awards. It is for the New Smart Car. This is the reader's problem: 'Parking in town is a nightmare, I need the smallest car possible.' And here is the solution: 'The New Smart Car is still so much smaller than other cars.'

Having identified the reason why people are interested in this car, all the team needed was a creative idea that dramatized or demonstrated that benefit. And here's what they did: they pictured the New Smart Car and, in a series of executions, drew a line underneath the picture which showed how much longer the competition's cars were.

And, bottom left, was the headline: 'New Smart for two. Still only 2.69 metres.'

It doesn't get any more basic than this, does it? Nor does it need to. What you have here is a clear presentation of the problem that the car solves for its owner.

Would you like another example?
If not, skip down to the next subhead.

This one comes out of a niche business-to-business brief aimed at long-distance truck drivers.

Here's their problem: 'When I'm driving at high speed, my main fear is losing control of the steering wheel because of poor roads or strong cross-winds.'

The solution: 'Volvo Dynamic Steering automatically regulates the steering to compensate for any unevenness that makes its way up the steering wheel as a result of side winds or potholes.'

If I were the owner of a haulage company, I'd be interested in what Volvo is saying. And year-on-year sales increases of 39 per cent in the European market, 57 per cent in South America and 17 per cent in the US suggest that many were impressed enough to buy a Volvo truck or two.[8]

However, the brilliance of the creative idea that dramatized the problem/solution guaranteed it a wider audience. If you haven't already seen it, then Google 'Volvo Epic Splits' now and join the eighty-four million other people who have watched the film.

While you are sitting there wide-eyed, listen for the second line of the voice-over: 'I've had my fair share of bumpy roads and strong winds,' which is a pretty bald statement of the problem. Then look out for the Super, which appears on screen a few seconds later: 'This test was set up to demonstrate the stability and precision of Volvo Dynamic Steering' – i.e., the solution to the problem.

What you can learn from the world's most successful brands

It's simple, isn't it? The prospect has a problem, and the product/service provides a solution – be it practical, like safe steering, or, as is often the case, psychological.

This problem/solution dynamic is at the core of all effective marketing communication. Indeed, the most successful brands can trace that success to their single-minded commitment to solving a key problem in their customers' lives.

For example, which brand achieved global domination by solving this problem: 'There is so much information out there on the web that I just do not know where to start.'

Yes, that's right, Google. Since Larry Page and Sergey Brin founded the company, its mission has been 'to organize the world's information and make it universally accessible and useful'.

Hence not only Google Search but also Street View, Maps, Flights, Autocorrect and Translate. All these proprietary tools are dramatizations and demonstrations of the original mission statement.

Google is a great example of how a company prospers

when it identifies how best it can serve its prospects and customers, and then sticks to its knitting. The second of its original ten guiding principles is, indeed, 'It's best to do one thing really, really well.'

It will be interesting to see how Google fares now it is diverting attention to such ventures as driverless cars, renewable energy, space exploration and Google Life Sciences. But that's Larry Page's conundrum, not ours.

Let's take a look at another power brand that, early in its existence, identified and then set out to address a key customer need. In this case, the problem can be paraphrased as: 'I strive to be the best I can be at [insert sport here], but I'm just not cutting it.'

And the answer? Nike's long-standing promise 'to bring inspiration and innovation to every athlete in the world'.

In the previous example, I suggested that Google's new ventures might be dangerous distractions. News that Nike is working on a sports-fashion line with the couture house Givenchy flashed a similar warning light. Then I read Riccardo Tisci, the creative director at Givenchy: 'A lot of the pieces are not sewn together, they are bonded or glued. Each gram, each extra bit of weight you eliminate in a garment, allows the body to perform better.'[9]

Seems like Nike is sticking to its knitting (or bonding and gluing) after all.

When you want people to notice your message, emulate these brands, and others like Amazon, Airbnb, Uber, Ebay and TripAdvisor. All have worked out that people are interested in what you say when you promise them something helpful.

Indeed, while such brands use increasingly sophisticated

digital tools to fulfil their promises, they know that success is rooted in a consumer insight.

So, before you start writing, get digging.

How to choose the right problem/solution

If you do enough spadework, then the one difficulty you'll have is this: you'll uncover too many ways your product/service/idea can help your prospect. When that happens, choose the one problem/solution dynamic that will impress the largest number of your most lucrative prospects.

This choice can be based on your own understanding of their needs. Or it could come from research, or how they have responded to past communications. If you can talk to the sales force about what turns the prospect on, then tap into their experience.

But be single-minded when it comes to choosing the problem/solution that will lie at the core of your message. (I'll explain what I mean by single-minded on page 39.)

How to deal with problem clients

If you're working with a client, then this may be the biggest headache you have: clients often ignore their customers' problems. Instead, many clients want the creative you produce to directly address *their* marketing problems.

It could be that 60 per cent of their customers have not yet signed up to pay by direct debit; or maybe their like-for-like sales are down 5 per cent this quarter. It might be that no one recognizes their packaging on the supermarket shelf, or that customers are redeeming their investments because fund management performance is poor.

These worries keep your client awake at night, and they like you to write copy that makes them go away.

If they demand this, then point out that their prospects and customers aren't tossing and turning at 4.00 a.m. over such issues. These people have their own problems. And it is your job to show them how the client's products can solve those problems – and get them to buy that solution.

Then explain to your client that if you can pull that off, their problems will be solved, too.

Alas, most agencies are loath to say this. So they deliver work that panders to the client and ignores the customer. Which leads to headlines like 'Tomorrow's Technology Today', 'The Best Just Got Better' and 'Expect the Unexpected'.

They're poor enough, but pride of place on the wall of shame goes to the ubiquitous 'The Art of . . .' I once opened an *Evening Standard* magazine and found three versions of this ad inside. I now have a collection of over a hundred, ranging from 'The Art of Christmas' to 'The Art of Summer' and 'The Art of Cashmere' to 'The Art of Stone Cladding'. Clients love this kind of self-referential tosh. Customers, however, rarely notice it.

Is this solving the wrong problem?

Here's another example that, despite its honourable intentions, looks like it was written to solve the client's problem.

Remember the Ice Bucket Challenge? In 2014 you couldn't move on social media without seeing some celebrity or other dumping a bucket of water over their head.

But if you live in the UK, you may be hard pressed to name the local charity behind the stunt. I couldn't until, almost twelve months after the craze began, I saw a poster at London Blackfriars railway station.

The visual featured the face of a handsome, stoic-looking man above the headline: '"**LAST SUMMER**, I WAS THE ONLY PERSON I KNEW WHO DIDN'T DO THE **ICE BUCKET CHALLENGE**. FIVE MONTHS LATER I WAS DIAGNOSED WITH MOTOR NEURONE DISEASE"—Michael, 34'. (The choice of capital letters and bold type is theirs.)

The body copy read: 'There is no cure for Michael's MND. There is very little time – 50% of people die within two years of diagnosis. But thanks to the Ice Bucket Challenge and the incredible awareness and understanding raised, there is now the knowledge they are not alone.'

And the call to action: 'You can read Michael's story and more at mndassociation.org #LastSummer'.

Which begs the initial question, why would I want to? And then the second, why were funds spent on this campaign?

My conclusion is that the folks at the charity were outpaced by the speed at which the Ice Bucket Challenge went viral. Months later they realized they'd missed out on much of the awareness and they were simply playing catch-up.*

Or maybe I'm being uncharitable.

Either way, while we're on the subject of charities,

---

* The MND Association is a well run and worthy charity. You can make a donation here: www.mndassociation.org/getinvolved/donations

there's a point I should make about problem/solution that's peculiar to that sector.

Why writing for a charity is different . . .

The way I've explained problem/solution thus far applies to all business-to-consumer and business-to-business communications.

But if you are writing for a charity, things are different. As we've seen, normally the problem is experienced by the reader and the solution is provided by the product or the service being advertised.

However, with charities, the dynamic changes.

Here the problem isn't experienced by the reader. It is experienced by the people or the cause the charity is trying to help. And that problem is the focus of the message.

In turn, the solution isn't provided by the advertiser. In charity ads, the solution comes from the reader, who is expected to help by giving money, time or some other donation.

. . . likewise social marketing

Things are also slightly different in social marketing campaigns. Typical examples might be the government's efforts to get people to stop smoking, or to start contributing to their workplace pension fund.

If the targeting is right, then here the problem resides with the reader. She is the one who is smoking, or facing a poverty-stricken retirement.

Likewise, the solution lies with her. Which means the

message must impress on the reader the need to change her behaviour, and therefore make the problem go away.

There's a fine example amongst this year's D&AD award winners. The advertisement's aim is to persuade seafarers always to wear a life jacket when they are on the water.

Like a lot of good work, it is based around a fact – in this case, that the average time a person can remain underwater before they inhale and lose consciousness is 87 seconds.

So the headline invites you to: HOLD YOUR BREATH AND READ THIS AD.

The body copy then takes you through the thoughts that might come into your head while holding your breath underwater for 19 seconds . . . 31 seconds . . . 43 seconds . . . 54 seconds . . . 58 seconds . . . 67 seconds . . . 78 seconds . . . 83 seconds . . . 85 seconds, and, finally and fatally, 87 seconds.

If the purpose of a creative idea is to dramatize or demonstrate a proposition, then this one works perfectly. Indeed, by the time you've finished reading you are doubled up in lung-scorching, eye-bulging agony.

What makes it even more effective is the way it plays to our survival instincts at the most fundamental and even primordial level. For, as you'll see on page 65, the old part of our brain is constantly alert to threats to our well-being.

As a species we also like to see our problems being solved. So, as with everything we write, working out the problem/ solution dynamic beforehand is vital. But, to borrow from Hamlet, such planning is usually 'more honoured in the breach than in the observance'.

Sorry if that quote seems a bit esoteric (indeed, sorry if esoteric seems a bit, well, esoteric – as we'll see in Chapter 7, it's advisable to keep references and vocabulary as simple as possible).

However, in quoting Shakespeare we come to another reason why problem/solution is an important starting point for your copy.

It is the basis for all storytelling – regardless of whether that story is about Henry V or iPhone 6.

Putting problem/solution at the heart of your story

In Henry V's case, the problem is the need to reclaim the throne of France for England; for Othello, it's his suspicion of his wife's infidelity; in *Romeo and Juliet* it is forbidden love and, going back to *Hamlet*, it's the young prince's need to avenge the murder of his father.

In his excellent book *Into the Woods: How Stories Work and Why We Tell Them*, John Yorke points out that in these and all other stories 'you have a central character, you empathize with them and something happens to them and that something is the genesis of the story . . . That something is almost always a problem . . . and the story is the journey they go on to sort out the problem presented.'[10]

As Yorke explains, the emergence of the problem, the search for a solution and the climactic resolution is the classic three-act structure around which pretty much all drama on TV, cinema and the theatre is built.

Make the reader your hero

What applies to *Breaking Bad* works just as well in the commercial stories that you and I write. The crucial difference is this: the central character of our copy is not a fictional chemistry teacher turned crystal meth dealer – it is the reader for whom we are writing.

It is the reader who has the problem. And it is our job to identify that problem right at the start. Then we have to introduce and describe the solution as provided by the product or service we are selling. And finally comes the resolution, wherein the reader discovers how they can enjoy the benefit of a life free of the problem they once had.

Like all stories, it has a beginning, a middle and an end, and it encompasses change.

And, as in all narrative forms, if the central character does not desire some kind of change, then as John Yorke says, 'they're passive. And if they're passive, they're effectively dead. Without a desire to animate a protagonist, the writer has no hope of bringing the character alive, no hope of telling a story and the work will almost always be boring.'[11]

Your reader is looking for solutions

A lot of the copy you read today is as dull as ditchwater precisely because no one has bothered to find out what the hero – the reader – wants. Which is a lost opportunity, because our readers are constantly on the lookout for solutions to the problems – big and small – that confront them.

As a species we cannot help it. We hate the randomness of our universe, and habitually tell ourselves stories that tidy up and explain away its unsatisfactory loose ends and dead ends. When it comes to the solutions that lie at the heart of those stories, usually we plump for the simplest. For example:

In our society, wealth is distributed unequally
– increase the top rate of income tax to 80 per cent.

Muslims aren't integrating into European society
– ban the burka.

American industry is uncompetitive – build a
2,500-mile wall between the US and Mexico.

My team has struggled recently – sack the Coach.

My marriage has gone a bit stale – have a fling.

I'm not as successful as I should be – blame my parents.

Most of the lads I know are getting more sex than I am
– wear Lynx aftershave.

Most of today's brand narratives are talking to themselves

As the last example indicates, if we look to brands for anything then it is their capacity to make our lives easier and more pleasant, i.e. to solve our problems – be they practical or psychological.

But, in their rush to ride the 'fourth wave of content marketing', brands have ignored this need. Instead they have trotted out their back-stories in the belief that the reader will care enough to interact.

However, their invitations to 'read our story here', and the countless web pages and videos based upon such content, go unseen, because there's nothing in there to which the audience can relate.

What's needed is a story that puts the reader at its core. Like this, from the website of a men's knitwear company called Mr Quintessential. Here's its founder explaining why he started the business: 'Mr Quintessential was born out of the idea that many things in my wardrobe looked too immature for my years. They say that men lose interest in fashion in their late thirties, but I strongly disagree. I still want to be stylish and look good. Even though I am well into middle age. I am too young to be old, and I am too old to dress in high street clothes, emblazoned with logos and initials. These items are just too risky for a man with grey in his hair.'

Now, I'd have preferred the piece to include the reader a little more overtly. I like copy that talks about 'you' rather than 'I' or 'we'. But here the writer has identified a problem that many middle-aged men share. And I think a lot of his readers will relate to what he says.

Once the rapport is established, the copy goes into factual detail about the quality of the clothing and concludes, 'Mr Q. will take you on a journey, an adventure in colour, and dress you in knitwear which is that little bit more grown up.'

Having described the problem earlier on, he tells his reader the 'little bit more grown up' solution that he has in store. Indeed, as you can see, he also refers to the 'journey' he is going to take the reader (his hero) on in the quest for that solution.

Such classic storytelling – and salesmanship – is unusual at a time when, according to Helen Edwards in *Marketing* magazine: 'the consumer is drowning in an ocean of branded pap.'[12]

This poor soul's problem is rarely identified. And, if it is, the second act of the drama, the solution, usually looks like it was dashed off by a writer with one eye on the clock and the other on a very tight word count.

As for the resolution, the call to action explaining how

the main character can get hold of the product or service being advertised – well, nowadays a lot of commercial copy cuts this completely.

So what's the reason for this state of affairs? Well, let's find out from the people who should know better than anyone: the copywriters who produce the work. As we're about to see, they're a demoralized bunch. But at least they've identified their problem – and where its solution lies.

3:

HOW TO WRITE YOUR BRIEF

Last year, the Direct Marketing Association held the first ever census of British copywriters. Four hundred and thirty-three responded. The findings appear in a book that would benefit from a spoiler alert. It's called *Why Your Copywriter Looks Sad*.

Apparently, copywriters are down in the dumps because a) no one is reading their work, and b) most of it isn't worth reading in the first place.

Why are those standards so low? Well, when asked 'What is the main barrier to good work?', 68 per cent of respondents said, 'Poor briefs.'

The answer to the follow-up question – 'What's the most important thing when it comes to helping you do better work?' – was even more emphatic. Seventy per cent replied: 'The clarity of the brief.'

I sympathize and empathize, and would have said exactly the same thing. At my agency, we spent twice as long on the brief as we did on the creative. We knew that if the brief wasn't right, the creative wouldn't be right either.

Such preparation was essential. When clients baulked at the time we took, I'd tell them about Abraham Lincoln's approach to problem-solving. He said: 'If I'm given six hours to chop down a tree, I'll spend four hours sharpening the axe.'

You should allocate your time in the same way. If you

have a deadline of six days, spend four of them writing your brief.

Your starting point should be your two questions about problem/solution. What come next are eight more questions, aimed at giving you a clear picture of what you are going to say to your reader.

Question 1: Who am I writing to, and how do they feel about the thing I'm selling?

Don't regard your target as a demographic code or profile. It doesn't help when it comes to writing to them. So avoid referring to 'empty nesters' or 'solitary survivors'. And don't reduce the reader to a label like ABC1 or Generation Y.

Think of your reader as an individual, but write about them only in the context of the thing you are selling. Ask yourself: have they bought the product/service before? If so, what have they bought, and how frequently?

This is important. It means you have a relationship, so don't treat them like a stranger. Don't try to *sell* them things – make your message more of a *suggestion* or *recommendation*, based on what they have bought from you in the past.

When you're writing the brief, you should also be clear about how they feel about the thing you are selling. Do they like it? Are they indifferent? And how important is it to the reader?

Sure, to you it's the greatest thing since the last greatest thing you had to sell. But as Bob Hoffman writes in *Marketers Are from Mars, Consumers Are from New Jersey*: 'The average consumer has other things on her mind. Like why she gained two pounds last week, and why her father is looking pale, and why the fucking computer keeps losing its WiFi signal, and why Timmy's teacher wants to see her next week, and what's that bump she noticed on her arm?"[1]

So, keep trying to see the product through her eyes. That way, your copy will ring true.

Finally, if they haven't bought from you before, then are they aware of the product/service you are selling? Do they buy it from others? If they don't buy from you or the competition, how are they getting by in life without it?

How business-to-business differs

If you are writing business-to-business, your prospect is probably not the ultimate decision-maker. And they may have to get permission from someone else before they can buy the thing you are selling.

If that's the case, acknowledge this other person's existence in the brief. Then make sure you provide your original prospect with all the information they need to sell the product/service on to their colleague.

It could be that the problem/solution that is driving this communication will also work for the person who is holding the purse strings. If it does, then fine. With a slight tweak to acknowledge their status, send your original prospect's communication to them.

Be warned, however: in business-to-business, one execution rarely works across different departments. Each prospect has their own problems, and you've got to identify them and work out how your product can solve them. Then write to each individual separately.

Question 2: What does your reader think about your brand?

Here's a question that applies to both business-to-consumer and business-to-business: if the product or service you are writing about has a well-developed brand, what does the prospect think about it?

Are you, for example, British Airways – established, professional and respected? Or are you Virgin Atlantic – disruptive, fun and liked?

Are you Barcelona FC – exciting, popular and populist? Or are you Real Madrid – rich, glamorous and corporate?

Are you Sofitel – luxurious, aspirational and expensive? Or are you Ibis – clean, cheap and convenient?

These guidelines help you find the correct tone of voice, and bring consistency to all the pieces of writing you do for this brand.

They'll also stop you making mistakes like this: recently, Airbnb was angry about the San Francisco legislature's plans to levy occupancy tax on the rooms they let in that city. So they ran a series of posters challenging the city to spend tax revenues wisely.

The ads went down like a fart in a crowded yoga class because Airbnb hadn't kept pace with the way the public saw them.

They were acting like an up-and-coming garage brand that could confront authority and start a groundswell of popular opinion. That might have worked in the early days, but not for a business with a market value exceeding $24 billion.

The public now saw Airbnb as a mega-corporation that was berating the city's cash-strapped public services and, by inference, moaning about having to pay the taxes that keep those public services running. Within days, Airbnb had taken the ads down and apologized for striking 'the wrong tone'.[2]

If you want to avoid making similar gaffes, make sure you are clear about how the brand you are promoting is perceived and how you want it to be portrayed.

But a word of warning: if the guidelines you need don't exist, please don't make them up because you think this gap on the brief should be filled. Coming up with brand positioning and identity is a bit more complex than that. Leave it blank, and move to the next question.

Question 3: What does your reader think before receiving this message?

First have another look at your problem/solution at the start of the brief. Then focus on the problem, and use this section to go into a bit more detail about that problem.

I know that sounds obvious, but I've seen smart people set up a great problem/solution at the start and then introduce something very different when they reach this part of the brief. So stay focused.

Suppose, for example, you are writing for a company called Turn Gold to Cash which promises to swap cash for the old jewellery that people send them.

Here is the prospect's problem: 'I'm struggling to make ends meet at the moment and would love to get my hands on some spare cash.'

And here's the solution offered by Turn Gold to Cash: 'If you have any old gold jewellery, coins or medals hanging round the house, send them to us and you can have cash in your hand within 48 hours.'

When you get to question 3, you then need about three or four sentences that give a bit more insight into this person's problem and how they feel about it: 'I'm struggling to make ends meet at the moment. Sure, I'm getting by, but I don't have any money if things go wrong. Nor do I have a nest egg I could dip into for a treat or a little luxury.'

We'll get round to an expanded version of the solution to this when we discuss question 4. But, for the time being, here are some more examples of how to write the 'What does the reader think before receiving this message?' bit.

Perhaps your prospect is a finance director of a medium-sized company: 'My biggest headache is getting paid by the people who owe our business money. There are millions of pounds outstanding. To keep on top of things and chase payment, I'm going to have to hire two more people in my Accounts Receivable team.'

Or you're writing to a senior person who can no longer use the stairs in their home: 'I've been here for forty-two years, but it's getting impossible for me to get up and down stairs to the toilet and to bed at night. It's heartbreaking to think I may have to leave here and move into sheltered accommodation.'

Or you're writing to a very rich hedge fund manager: 'I work crazy hours and spend very little time with my wife and kids. I don't want to fail them or be a stranger to them. In fact, I want them to see me as the best dad they could have.'

Question 4: What do you want your reader to think after they have received this message?

Once again, make sure you've looked at the problem/solution that appears at the start of your brief. But this time, take the opportunity to elaborate on the solution.

For example, to the person who is struggling to get their hands on some cash you might write: 'That's great. I've got a locket and chain I never wear, a bracelet that's broken and the eternity ring that two-timing Tim gave me. If I send them off to Turn Gold to Cash today, they'll buy them off me and in two days' time I'll have extra money to spend.'

Or to the finance director who is struggling with his debtors: 'This new Eureka software has cut Day Sales Outstanding by 25 per cent for such companies as John Lewis and Vodafone. It does automatically within minutes what it would take a member of my team half a day to accomplish.'

Or for the elderly woman whose main fear is having to leave the place where she's lived for over forty years: 'A Stayhome Stair Lift would be just the job. Once it's installed, I can zip up and down the stairs whenever I want to, and there'll be no need for me to leave the home I love.'

And finally, for the hedge fund manager who is trying to find time for his wife and kids: 'This is very useful. Brown + Hudson Travel will tailor a bespoke holiday for me and the family. It will give me and the kids the chance to see, do and share extraordinary things together, and leave them with experiences they'll remember forever.'

Clearly, what is being sold here is not merely a holiday. Nor, in fact, is Brown + Hudson simply giving this Master of the Universe a means of assuaging his guilt about neglecting his family. No, the bespoke travel company is offering this most competitive of individuals a lasting hold on his children's affections, and the chance to be a better dad than all his kids' friends' parents.

Question 5: What do you want your reader to do?

To be honest, you should have thought of this before now, because the answer will determine which media you use.

Should you want existing customers to know about your end-of-season sale, then something short and highly targeted like a tweet or a text might do the trick.

If, however, you want them to upgrade to a more expensive product, then use an email or a letter. Both will give you the space you need to persuade your customer that the added cost of upgrading is worth it in terms of the advantages it brings. Moreover, you have an existing relationship with this person, and emails or letters are good media for strengthening that bond.

Alternatively, if you want prospects to enquire so you can build a new list of leads, then a press ad or Facebook ad might deliver for you.

Whichever medium you choose, make sure you are very clear about the objective. Remember you're describing what you want the reader to do after receiving this message. And there is only so much a single communication can achieve – so please be realistic.

It might be one of these: go to the website or call us now and buy the product. Phone for more information. Add this to your shopping cart. Return the coupon for a free sample.

Hand in this voucher at the check-out. Share this with a friend. Look for our product when you go into the super-market. Email to arrange a meeting. Be ready for our phone call.

Question 6: What proposition are you making to your reader?

For me, this is the most challenging but ultimately satisfying part of not just the brief, but the creative process. It is the promise that will make your reader take notice of your message, and get them to engage with what you are saying.

It comes directly out of the problem/solution dynamic that you identified at the start of your brief and expanded on in questions 3 and 4.

In short, it is the advantage they will get from using the product or service you are selling.

Here's how to phrase it. Imagine you are on the third floor of your building and you are leaving for the evening. You call for the lift and, when the doors open, inside is the personification of all your prospects.

You now have eleven seconds before the lift reaches the ground floor. What are you going to say to them that will get the reply: 'Bloody hell, that'd be useful, tell me more?'

Here are some examples based on the people we met in questions 3 and 4

If you are in the lift with the person who is hard up for cash, your promise might be:

'Send us your old, broken or unwanted gold jewellery,

and you can have ready cash in your hand in less than 48 hours.'

Or if the occupant of the lift is the finance director who is chasing the company's debtors:

'When you start using our new software, you can cut your Day Sales Outstanding by 25%.'

How about the woman who doesn't want to be forced out of her home?

'With a Stayhome Stair Lift to whisk you up and down the stairs, you can stay in the home you love for as long as you like.'

And finally, the hedge-fund supremo who wants to be the best father in the world:

'For your next holiday, treat your family to an experience *your* children will tell *their* children about.'

Please note than none of these propositions are written as clever turns of phrase. They haven't been 'spun' in the manner of most headlines. Most just follow the simple structure: if you do this then you will get this benefit.

As we will see on page 113, this simple combination of cause and effect is a fundamental of storytelling. But more of that later.

As I said, these propositions aren't clever, and they haven't been spun. They are just clear expressions of what's in it for the reader. As such, you could run them as the headline on your web page, press ad, poster or brochure; or you could pop them in as the over line to your direct mail letters or, in cut-down form, your subject lines in emails.

You could also tweet them, like Richard Branson does. He goes to great lengths to boil all his thinking down to 140 characters or fewer. As he explains: 'In anything I write

I now make a conscious effort to condense the point I want to make into a Twitter-like format.'[3]

Branson learned the value of the pithy, punchy proposition from the entrepreneur he respects most: Steve Jobs. When Jobs was launching a product, he would agonize over the single sentence that summed up its key benefit. For him, it was time well spent: 'Simple can be harder than complex: you have to work hard to get your thinking clean to make it simple. But it's worth it in the end because once you get there, you can move mountains.'[4]

Be single-minded

Like Steve Jobs, you should strive for the single-minded proposition.

Now, initially this may sound pretty simple. But the hardest thing you'll have to do here is keep your proposition down to one promise. There is always the temptation to sneak in another benefit.

Take the first example we saw: if you are greedy you might want to tack another benefit on there at the end: 'Send us your old, broken or unwanted gold jewellery and you can have ready cash in your hand in less than 48 hours – reassured by the fact that *Which* magazine say we're the UK's most trusted cash-for-gold buyer.'

Can you see where this starts getting complicated? Is the key message to the prospect about a) getting cash quickly, or is it b) the reassurance of knowing you aren't going to run off with their gold?

If you opt for the latter then you've moved on to a very different problem/solution – and you're going to have to start again.

Whichever you choose, you have to be single-minded and focus on the one benefit. However, when you face this dilemma, don't worry about not being able to talk about the other ways you can help the prospect. As we'll see when we get to question 8, there's room for that, too.

But before we get there, let's look at question 7.

Question 7: How do you back up the promise you've just made?

If you've got the reader to say, 'Bloody hell, that'd be useful, tell me more', you can't fob them off with an instruction to look at your website. They won't. And you'll have wasted a hard-earned opportunity to persuade them to do what you want them to do.

No, at this moment, they want to hear the hard facts that back up the claim you've made.

So, in this section of the brief, you explain exactly how you'll deliver on your promise. And that means describing how your product or service works.

People like this kind of detail. According to a recent study by KPMG Nunwood, the brands that excel in consumers' eyes are those that make a point of knowing their stuff and sharing it openly with their customers. As David Conway, director of Nunwood, says, 'The organizations that do well tend to be the ones that are hugely knowledgeable and put the consumer in control.'[5]

But sharing what you know is just the start.

If someone else has said things that support the promise you're making, then capture those comments here. It might be a review posted by a respected blogger or trade publication. It could be an award that you've won, praise that's been heaped on your product or service by an industry body, or a regular appearance atop the best-buy tables.

On the subject of accolades, there are some that are particularly useful if you are selling direct from the web. There are lots of cowboys trading in the virtual marketplace. So, prove you are one of the good guys by displaying any e-commerce awards, trade or web association logos or other kitemarks you have.

But back to selling, and if an independent body has run like-for-like tests against the competition and you've come out on top, then include that data here. And if no one has been so obliging, organize your own tests, then get them verified by a respected third party.

As you'll see in Chapter 6, people also like the reassurance of knowing that the claim you've made is not only true but also that the benefit is already being enjoyed by others. So it is very important that you include case studies and testimonials from satisfied customers.

Facts beat flannel every time

When you are trying to make your point, there is no substitute for facts. I learned this back in the late eighties, when I started as a copywriter. However, this lesson came from someone much more formidable than any creative director I ever had.

It was the weekly mugging the then Prime Minister, Margaret Thatcher, gave to her opponent on the Opposition benches at Prime Minister's Question Time. Take a look at these encounters on YouTube.

You'll see Neil Kinnock, speaking passionately with few

notes and even fewer doubts about the righteousness of his cause. Then you'll watch Mrs T. step up to the dispatch box, brandishing the stats with which she swats her opponent aside.

A fistful of facts always beats bombast and bluster.

This lesson is being applied by the current government's Behavioural Insights Team (or 'nudge unit') to problems in the National Health Service. For example, in the past, the NHS tried to persuade people to be 'fair to others' and phone in when they couldn't make it to a hospital appointment. Such appeals to the reader's better nature had little impact. But telling patients that their failure to attend costs the NHS £160 has reduced the level of missed appointments by almost a quarter.

The 'nudge unit' is also helping the Inland Revenue use hard facts to wield soft power. On their advice, the Revenue has stopped making vague threats about the severe and condign punishment of late payers. Instead they explain that if the taxpayer coughs up on time then the tax revenues will be used to pay for named projects in the taxpayer's locale. Thus appealing to the reader's self-interest by describing the specific benefit she'll enjoy.

Question 8: Which of your reader's other problems will your product/service solve?

I've stressed the need for you to focus on a single-minded proposition. And, if you're writing a poster, banner, tweet or text then there'll only be room to communicate the one key benefit that's been described in your promise (question 6).

However, media like emails, letters, press ads, brochures,

e-zines, websites and microsites give you more room. And this means you can lead with the main promise *and* then tell your reader the other reasons why they'll be better off with what you are selling.

But, as before, make sure you describe your reasoning in terms of the reader's problems and the solutions you are bringing.

Don't write a list of features. By that I mean what the product or service does. Think about these features in terms of the benefits they bring to the reader. Then explain them in that way.

Once the brief is finished, make sure everyone agrees with it

If you are writing for yourself, and no one else needs to be consulted, then so far, so good.

But if you're working with clients, then they might have their own ideas about the thrust of your message. Indeed, they may want you to focus on something that you think is of little interest to the reader. For example, remember what we said on page 19 about them wanting you to solve their problems and not the prospect's?

When that happens, you will need to persuade them that yours is the better approach.

If this discussion takes place *after* you've written your copy then you've wasted days of hard work. If you have to start again, you probably won't have time to do the job properly. Then you risk missing the deadline. And, as a result, your client may not want to pay you.

So it's best to discuss the brief *before* you start writing it.

Make sure your client understands how important it is to the success of the project. Then discuss with them the problem/solution and the proposition.

Once the brief is written, try to take them through it face to face. If you have to email it, make sure you phone them and explain your thinking.

Either way, get them to sign it off. That's right, get their signature. That way, it's as much their brief as it is yours. What's more, they then know what the work will be about even before it is written – which, in turn, will make it a lot easier to sell when that time comes.

I cannot give enough emphasis to the importance of your brief. It's your satnav on the road to clear communication.

4:

GETTING YOUR MESSAGE IN THE RIGHT ORDER

OK, you've got your brief sorted out. Well done. You've just given yourself a big advantage over the competition. For, as the woebegone writers told us on page 29, few get the luxury of a tight brief.

Having that brief does not, however, mean you are ready to start banging out the copy. Now you need to plan the order in which your story will appear.

We touched on this when we looked at the three-act structure:

Act 1: The reader's problem.

Act 2: The solution that's provided by the thing you are selling, or the idea you are proposing.

Act 3: The resolution, or what the reader must do in order to get hold of the thing you are selling or adopt the idea you are proposing.

If you're writing short copy, you could start with this as your guide. But for anything else, you'll need to structure your argument. And the best way of doing this is to use something that goes by the acronym AIDCA.

It stands for Attention, Interest, Desire, Conviction and Action. When I started as a copywriter, such was the perceived wisdom enshrined in those five words that AIDCA was passed on to me as if it was a gospel truth.

Indeed, given the enduring importance of AIDCA, you can imagine how pleased I was when, in researching this book, I unearthed what looked like the copywriting equivalent of the *Codex Sinaiticus*.

The origins of AIDCA

Just over a hundred years ago, Business Books Ltd of Whitefriars House, Tallis Street, London EC4 published the *Encyclopedia of Advertising and Selling*.

No author was cited, yet whoever wrote this book nailed what became the classic structure for a sales argument. While the emphasis is mine, here is what was written in 1915:

1) The opening which wins the reader's *attention* and prompts them to go further into the letter.

2) Description and explanation that gains *interest* by picturing the position in their mind.

3) Argument or proof, which creates *desire* for the article you have to sell by showing its value and advantages.

4) Persuasion, which draws the reader to your way of thinking by showing the adaptation of the article to his needs and his need of it now.

5) Inducement, which gives him particular or extra reason for buying.

6) The climax, which makes it easy for the reader to order and *prompts him to act* at once.

As far as AIDCA is concerned, all I need add is that 4) and 5) provide the Conviction.

As the anonymous writer went on to explain, you can use this structure for any piece of writing that's aimed at persuading people to do what you want them to do.

Of course, not all the elements need appear in everything you write. But if you are proposing a product, service or idea that your reader might, in some way, resist, then I'd advise you to use AIDCA.

Anticipate your reader's resistance

I've just referred to your reader's resistance. When you are working out the structure of your argument, factor it into your thinking. Then ask 'what are the obstacles I have to overcome in order to get them to say "yes"?'

For example, imagine if, after you've read this book, I want you to meet me for a beer next time you are in London. If I write you an email about this, then the journey from A to B should be a short, flat path.

If, on the other hand, I want you to hire me to write your copy at an exorbitant £1,000 a day, then I'll have to overcome much stronger resistance on your part. And getting you from A to B will be quite an obstacle course.

Whichever it is, I must anticipate my reader's reactions, and work out how to overcome them.

In so doing, I'll be able to answer the ancient conundrum:

How long should your copy be?

If it's appearing on the web, then the conventional wisdom says it needs to be shorter than if it's in print.

Yet, according to the respected writer and teacher Andy Maslen, 'one of the biggest, and most persistent, myths surrounding online copy is that it has to be short. Evidence is rarely provided to support this assertion. The writers usually prefer vague statements such as, "people get tired reading online". Or, even less convincingly, "people won't read long copy on the web".'[1]

Maslen's view is validated by the proliferation of long-form content on the web. Neil Patel, who is a star writer for the Content Marketing Institute, certainly has no qualms about writing beyond the fold. For him, 'long form content persuades better, converts better, shares better, ranks better and is better'. And when he says 'long form content', he means 3,000 words or more.[2]

Whatever your opinion, I suggest you follow Howard Gossage's advice. 'Use just enough string to wrap the parcel.'[3] For example, if it's a small parcel containing the message: 'Meet me for a beer next time you're in London,' a short string of words will do.

If a big box is needed to hold the message – 'Hire me to write your copy at £1,000 a day' – then a long string of words will be called for.

The length of your copy also depends on whether you are looking for a direct sale or whether you just want a lead.

For example, suppose I want you to hire me to write your copy and I want a direct sale – that is, I want you to send me a brief to start working immediately. My initial email will have to explain all the advantages I can bring you. Moreover, it will have to anticipate your many reasonable doubts, and try to overcome them.

Alternatively, I may just want you to call me to chat about the possibility of us working together. In which case, there will be fewer obstacles to overcome and the email can be shorter.

Of course, that's all hypothetical nonsense. You won't need me, or anyone else, to write your copy because you'll soon be able to do it all yourself.

Especially as we've now done all the prep work and we're about to start on the writing.

5:

HOW TO WRITE YOUR HEADLINE

So, you have your brief by your side, and your plan for how your message will play out.

Whether you're writing a web page or an email, a brochure or a press ad, the thing you need now is a headline.

Or do you? I ask because a lot of people in advertising disagree.

For example, this year the D&AD gave Press and Writing for Advertising awards to ads which had no headlines, just solid blocks of type.

The judges at Cannes trumped this by giving Press Lions to several headless wonders, and to ads for Pepsi that had no headline, body copy, strapline or logo.

The situation is just as absurd when it comes to posters.

Most now conform to the fashionable view of the perfect ad layout, with the headline reduced to a tiny and indiscernible design element – or removed completely – leaving just the visual and the logo.

This means it's increasingly unlikely you will win a Press or Poster award at Cannes, D&AD, or any of the other major advertising award shows – unless you follow the minimalist formula.

Why a headline is essential

I think that formula is wrong, and I have some formidable allies on my side.

My first is David Ogilvy – a copywriter and agency chief whose face should be carved on the Mount Rushmore of advertising greatness.

As the old boy said: 'On average, five times as many people read the headline as read the body copy. When you have written your headline, you have spent eighty cents of your dollar. If you haven't done some selling in your headline, you've wasted 80 per cent of your client's money. The wickedest of all sins is to run an advertisement without a headline.'[1]

Of course, that was over thirty years ago and the world has changed, hasn't it?

Well, according to Jakob Nielsen, who knows more about writing for the web than anyone, 'By far the most important thing you can do to help users consume content is to make use of meaningful headings, and make these headings visually pop as compared to body copy.'[2]

That other expert on web design, Steve Krug, is also for headlines, or clear 'visual hierarchies', as he calls them.[3] Both men say that headlines that *look* like headlines, i.e. big and bold, are the best way to capture the attention of readers who are scanning or skimming onscreen copy.

Incidentally, Nielsen and Krug suggest that this initial superficial sweep is peculiar to the way people read from their laptops, tablets and mobiles.

It isn't. Professor Siegfried Vögele pioneered the use of eye-scanning research in the 1970s and, back then, described the split-second 'reading curve' with which the reader assessed whether a page might be worth a second look.[4]

Vögele's speciality was direct mail, but everything he said about the reader's skimming of the page applies to all the types of commercial copy that you'll be writing.

So, too, does his advice on using headlines to telegraph your message and help your reader get into the copy.

This telegraphing via a headline isn't just a tactic used in advertising. It is a fundamental of storytelling. It is certainly advocated by the world's most successful storyteller, the creator of *Star Wars*, George Lucas.

He advises budding screenwriters to 'start with one sentence' and explains that 'a tagline is a one-sentence description of the idea you have. It's a "hook", a catchphrase, something that is memorable and will leave your readers wanting more. It's a phrase that conveys the very foundation of your story in as few words as possible . . . Here's a classic example of a tagline from the movie *Alien*: "In space, no one can hear you scream." This tagline works as a dramatic sentence that conveys the tone and setting for the film and it paints a chilling scene from a space horror.'[5]

Give your reader vital cues

What Lucas says about his taglines applies to your headlines. And, as he implies, your readers don't just rely on your headline as a quick and easy way to spot an interesting story – the headline's job is more fundamental than that.

It plays a vital part in setting the scene or framing the story that is about to be played out. Cognitive psychologists call these mental constructs 'schemata'. They are important in every aspect of our lives, for they help us make sense of our surroundings, telling us what to expect from life and how to behave.

If, for instance, you visit a client, your initial experience will help you find the schema that will thereafter guide your actions. To begin with, you'll recognize familiar things like offices and people going about their work in the background. In the foreground there'll be a reception area with someone at a desk who'll greet you, offer you a coffee and invite you to sit in the area reserved for those who, like you, are waiting for appointments.

All of the above cues will help you locate your schema marked 'office life'. And this schema lets you know there's no point in asking for a pint of beer, or trying to put £5 each way on Breezy Boy in the 3.15 at Wincanton. No, your schema tells you to check your emails or quietly pretend to read that *FT* on the table in front of you.

This, and hundreds of other schemata, help us negotiate everyday life. If we didn't have them, we'd have to process information anew at every point in our existence. As a result, our brains would need to be much larger than they are now, and the human race would have died out millennia ago because our craniums would have been too big for natural childbirth.

Use a schema to pull people into your copy

As I said on page 7, reading is hard work. Coming to your squiggles cold, your target will have no idea what they mean. So, as they scan the page or the screen, they are searching for cues which will allow them to find a schema.

Once they have that schema, they start figuring out your story.

As Yellowlees Douglas says in *The Reader's Brain*: 'The titles of articles or books, their author names, and other details . . . cue schemas that help us to narrow considerably the range of inferences we need to make as we read.'[6]

She could also have included your headlines in this list. And, for that matter, subheads, straplines under your logo, captions under your photographs and postscripts on letters. All of these enable the reader to create a schema which, according to Douglas, provides them 'with a clear blueprint of exactly where all those printed pages are headed'.[7]

For example, suppose you're writing about whisky. If the reader sees prominent words that he associates with the topic, he'll be primed for what's coming.

Now I am not suggesting that you shoehorn such words in where they do not fit. However, reference in headlines, subheads and captions to things like 'single malt', 'distillery', 'peat', 'aged 12 years' help to set the mental scene. In so doing, they also allow the reader to anticipate what's coming next, which, as we'll see, is the path to understanding.

Alternatively, if you run a web page, a press ad or a brochure without a headline, you are wilfully limiting the reader's ability to understand your meaning. And that's as dumb as refusing to turn on the electric light while you are searching for your house keys in a dark room.

Use abruption to get your headline noticed

We've seen that there are three qualities that get your headline noticed. Putting news into the line will attract readers.

So will a phrase or sentence that arouses their curiosity. Both are fine. But nothing beats a benefit.

However, even then you might struggle to catch your prospect's eye.

After all, they're only scanning the screen or page where your work appears. And there are thousands of other messages vying for their attention. So you might need something else.

There's a term for that something. It is 'relevant abruption', and here's what it means:

Relevant abruption is a sudden and unexpected impact that draws your reader's attention to the advantage they'll get from the product or service you are selling.

Why and how does this work?

Well let's start with the abruption – 'the sudden and unexpected impact'. To understand its potency, let's go back to page 13 and what we said about the basic human instincts that attract us to the novel and the unknown.

According to Harvard psychologist Deirdre Barrett, those instincts 'were designed for hunting and gathering on the savannahs of Africa 10,000 years ago, and they would guide us to healthy behaviours if we were still on the savannahs'.[8]

Alas, we are not. And our instincts haven't adjusted to our change of address. But, as Barrett points out, our 'orienting influence' still works as if we were wandering the wilderness on the lookout for new and unknown threats.

As she says, 'the orienting influence is when you see something novel, your reflexive response is to turn your head toward it, focus on it, still the rest of your body and just pay attention for a split second and see if it's something that you need to evaluate more.'[9]

Much of what we see in today's entertainment and media landscape is aimed at tweaking the orienting influence with ever-more-novel stimuli. Indeed, these attempts to exploit one of our most basic instincts explain everything from Lady Gaga's constantly changing couture to Daesh's disgusting videos.

If you are to compete for your reader's attention then you, too, should try to say something that's out of the ordinary. That makes people look twice. That activates the orienting influence.

But please, exercise this option with care.

Make sure it's relevant

If you write 'TITS' at the top of your web page, you may well get your prospect's attention. But unless yours is the RSPB's website, then it is unlikely the reader will think too highly of you once they realize you've duped them into stopping on your page.

Indeed, when next they see your logo they'll dismiss it, and your message will not register.

And nor will your cash registers ring – as Benetton discovered. Years of shocking posters did nothing for their sales once the public realized those abruptive images had bugger all to do with chunky knit sweaters.

So your abruptive headline must also be relevant: it must draw the reader's attention to either the problem they are encountering or the solution you are providing, and thus the advantage you are offering. And even then, you need to be careful how far you go in trying to be abruptive.

Take, for example, this ad from Singapore retailer Super-

Gurl. Next to a visual of a distressed-looking teenager they ran the headline: 'Black Friday Sale – Rape us now'. Yes, it got noticed, but for all the woefully wrong reasons.

Compare that with another headline that tweaked our innate fascination with the new, the novel and the downright sensational.

Here's a good example

It is about a six-year-old boy called Harrison who has Duchenne Muscular Disorder. The boy's father knows the disease has no cure and, unlike even the most devastating cancers, there is no treatment for it.

This made him determined to raise money for research and he started working with the agency AIS on a fundraising advertisement. The agency did exactly as they should and spent hours with the father listening to the facts and how he was feeling.

As the father said, 'During the creative process, the agency asked me to take them through Harrison's diagnosis, tap into the dark thoughts I had and be brutally honest about what I felt. We covered everything from start to finish – even so far as describing the corridor outside the consultant's room where we stood motionless while Harrison ran around post-diagnosis. I quietly told them I wish my son had cancer.'[10]

And that thought, unspun and unmediated by the creative team, became the headline to the advertisement.

I cannot think of a more abruptive headline than 'I wish my son had cancer.' Not surprisingly, it got a huge response – both positive and negative.

A lot of people complained that the ad was insensitive to those with cancer. But to my mind, it was a valid use of shock tactics. It genuinely described the way Harrison's father was feeling. There was a rawness to his words that no copywriter could conjure. And they got the results he was looking for.

From this single 25×4 ad he raised £65,000, and £200,000 over the calendar year in which it ran.

Moreover, he was invited to appear on such TV shows as *ITV London News* and *BBC Breakfast*. Various local BBC radio stations interviewed the family, and the World Service sent the story round the world, with newspapers as far away as Brazil picking it up. Back home, Harrison featured in the *Daily Mail*, the *Independent* and the *Guardian*. All of which equated to hundreds of thousands of pounds in free commercial air time and press coverage for the charity.

Needless to say, visits to the Harrison website were frequent, and Facebook reach grew massively.

Admittedly, some of the comments on social media were harsh. But when you say something abruptive like this, you must accept you'll be attacked on grounds of taste, decency or whatever accusations are levelled at you. However, if your message is relevant and draws attention to the benefit your product provides or the charity you are trying to support, grit your teeth and carry on.

Let's look at a few more headlines, and see how relevant abruption worked for them.

Five more examples of effective headlines

M&G Investments

Before we start, I should say that this advice is aimed not at creative teams who use words *and images* to communicate.

This is a guide to writing copy. So it is for those noble craftspeople, the copywriters, who rely upon headlines alone to grab their prospect's attention.

But even if you have the luxury of a visual and you're working with the most gifted art director or designer, you'll still need a good line. So maybe you should read on.

Let's start with this one from M&G Investments. They sell funds that deal in stocks and shares. But at the time this headline ran, they weren't selling many. The FTSE 100 had collapsed to 3,200. (If that doesn't mean much to you then, as I write, the FTSE 100 stands at 6,580.)

Anyway, it was at its lowest point in twenty years and M&G's customers and prospects were scared to death about losing their shirts (trousers, shoes and underwear).

Here's their problem/solution:

Problem: 'The markets are in freefall. Like everyone else, I'm panicking. Shouldn't I get out before I lose everything?'

Solution: 'The shrewd investor knows that the time to buy is when the markets are reaching the bottom. And right now we can help you make a killing.'

And here is the headline from the resulting press ad:

**In our opinion, there's
never ever been a
better time to invest
in the stockmarket***

That asterisk led the reader to a caption at the bottom of the page which read: 'If you don't count December 1973, that is. Remember Ted Heath? Three-day weeks? Power cuts? Back then, the stockmarket plummeted to an all-time low – thanks to an unprecedented rise in oil prices. But within two years, it had regained its original value and continued to rise.'

How's that for singling out your target audience? The ad was aimed at people over the age of 55 (in the UK, they account for more than 70 per cent of disposable income) and the references to 1973, Ted Heath, three-day weeks and power cuts homed in on, and spoke directly to, that segment.

Surrounding this were 820 words explaining that there were some fabulous bargains to be had. You just had to be level-headed enough to take advantage of the rock-bottom share prices.

This message was targeted at its affluent audience via a full-page advertisement in the main sections of the *Daily Telegraph* and the *Daily Mail*. By 10.00 p.m. on launch day, the BBC had contacted M&G's sales manager inviting him to justify such potentially ruinous advice on that evening's *Newsnight* programme.

Such is the power of a relevant abruption. Not only does it get your ad noticed, but in M&G's case, it got them twelve minutes of free commercial air time in which to attract new prospects and reassure old customers with the basic tenet of investing: buy low, sell high.

At a time of panic, the ad also had the invaluable effect of reassuring existing investors, and attracting several thousand new ones who wished to take up M&G's offer of their 'Spin-Free Guide to Investing'.

Here's another example of relevant abruption in a headline. It's from *The Economist*'s hugely successful poster campaign, and comes from the pen of the best English copywriter of his generation, David Abbott.

The target here is ambitious business executives.

Their problem: 'I'm determined to climb to the top of the corporate ladder, but the competition is tough; how do I get ahead of the rest?'

The solution: 'The business intelligence in *The Economist* gives you the advantage over your peers.'

And the poster headline that brought all this to life?

I never read The Economist

Management Trainee. Aged 42.

The line works because we assume that advertising will actively promote the product being sold. Yet this headline confounds this expectation, and begs the question: why is *The Economist* running such a negative comment about itself?

As John Yorke notes in *Into the Woods*, headlines like these demonstrate 'a basic narrative technique which forces you to read the copy underneath in hope that it will explain such a superficially strange juxtaposition'. It would appear that not much force is needed. For, as Yorke then explains, humankind is naturally inclined to reconcile such conflicting elements and seek resolution. We hate disorder and want our stories to end neatly.[11]

So we look closer at the line to see the small print beneath the quote, and smile to ourselves when we work out that it's the forty-two-year-old loser who is making the comment and not *The Economist* itself.

The loser represents the problem. The solution is provided by *The Economist*. And, as the reader infers, the resolution comes with a subscription.

Wall Street English

Here's another headline aimed at ambitious people. This time, the target is young people in Southeast Asia who are keen on learning English but have failed up until now because they lack the confidence to speak out in class. In their culture, to make mistakes is to lose face, and that's something few are willing to risk.

Wall Street English, however, has entered the market with a methodology specifically designed to help them overcome such inhibitions. Here's how it plays out:

Problem: 'I'd like to learn to speak English, but I am too shy to speak in class.'

Solution: 'We have a new method that builds your confidence and minimizes embarrassment.'

And the headline that communicates the benefit to the prospect?

Here's a new way to speak English
for those who've always been too shy to try

What makes this line abruptive? The news it conveys. The words 'Here's' and 'new' tick those boxes very nicely. You could put 'Now', 'Announcing', 'Introducing' or 'At last' in there instead of 'Here's', and you'd have the same impact.

See, also, how the headline addresses the target not once but twice. First, 'a new way to speak English' speaks directly to those who are in the market for such schooling. And then it shouts its relevance with direct reference to their problem: 'who've always been too shy to try'.

I hope this shows the appeal of news. If you are still in any doubt, have a stroll over to your fridge and look inside.

What Unilever can teach you about the value of news

The likes of Unilever, Kraft Heinz and Procter & Gamble have known for years that there's a sure-fire way of shifting product from supermarket shelves. They slap NEW onto their packaging. Yes, they are constantly tinkering with their existing product lines in order to add a NEW variant and retain customer interest. But they also do it when the product itself is the same as it has been for years.

A NEW size or a NEW pack or a NEW way of pouring the contents will attract customers simply because, well, they're NEW.

But bear with me a second; it's Saturday morning, and I must take a break and assume my duties as chief breakfast-maker for my fiancée, Morag.

I fancy some toast, so I pull out our loaf of Hovis Seed Sensations Original, which I note is 'NEW IMPROVED'. I'd like some cheese on that, but can't decide whether to go hard with Pilgrim's Choice Mature English Cheddar with the 'NEW LOOK – SAME GREAT TASTE', or soft with Philadelphia Cream Cheese ('NOW EVEN CREAMIER').

I opt for the latter, and drizzle some Il Casolere Extra Virgin Olive Oil which I notice is 'BEST POURING WITH

OUR NEW DISPENSER'. Mo said she wants cereal, so I mix her a bowl of 'NEW LOOK' Quaker Oats Oat Granola with some Special K from its 'NEW BIGGER PACK' and take that up to her with a mug of Douwe Egbert's Classic Roast coffee with its 'NEW RICHER TASTE'.

And so Mo and I tuck into our 'new', 'improved' breakfast. And, although we think we're wise to the wiles of P&G and Unilever, we cannot help the choices we make, for our shopping list was written 10,000 years ago by the old part of our brain.

We've seen how it is drawn to the new and the novel. Now let's look at how it also leads us to the grim and the grisly.

Le Musée de la Grande Guerre

We've had abruptive headlines that highlight benefits and the last one which majors on news. Now for one that arouses curiosity.

It's for a small museum in the French town of Meaux. Not surprisingly, given its location on the banks of the River Marne, the museum is dedicated to World War I.

The targets here are visitors to the region who need to be attracted to spend an afternoon at the Musée de la Grande Guerre.

Their problem: I have some free time. Meaux has a cathedral, an old quarter and Brie cheese, but what else is there to do?

The solution: Between 1914 and 1918, Meaux was on the front line of the most horrific war in history. Come and experience hell on earth at our museum.

And here's the headline that encapsulates those thoughts:

**Verdun. 26 million shells
or 6 per square metre.
Mathematically speaking,
even before the battle
you were already dead.**

Someone has clearly done their homework here. And I advise you to follow their lead. Because you often find the abruptive aspect of your headline amongst the facts you uncover during your background reading.

In this case, chilling statistics conjure the most horrific images and, in me at least, elicit the response: 'Bloody hell, that's incredible, tell me more.'

Indeed, if I was in Meaux for the day then morbid fascination would guarantee I spend a couple of hours in that museum. And I wouldn't be alone in being drawn to its scenes of death and destruction. For, once again, we see our most basic instincts coming to the fore – and a headline writer who understands how to play to them.

Susan M. Weinschenk explains why such headlines work – and why we're innately attracted to gruesome sights – in her book *100 Things Every Designer Needs to Know about People*: 'Have you ever wondered why traffic always slows when people are driving by an accident? . . . Well, it's not really your fault that you (and everybody else) can't resist looking at scenes of danger. It's your old brain telling you to PAY ATTENTION.'[12]

Dixons

That last advertisement also begs the question, is it OK to use long headlines? A lot of copywriters who work in agencies don't think so. Their aim is to reduce everything to the minimum. But in doing so, they often obscure what they are trying to say.

Here's a headline from award-winning copywriter Simon Dicketts, who clearly has no such hang-ups. It is for the electronics retailer Dixons, and from the headline alone, it is easy to work out the problem/solution.

> **Get off at the fashionable end**
> **of Oxford Street, drift into the**
> **achingly cool technology hall**
> **of London's most happening**
> **department store and view**
> **this year's must-have plasma**
> **courtesy of the sound and vision**
> **technologist in the Marc Jacobs**
> **sandals. Then go to dixons.co.uk**
> **and buy it**

What makes this headline abruptive? Its attitude. We don't expect advertisers to tell us to be so downright sneaky. Nor do we often encounter advertising that understands us so well.

But, as I've said throughout, the primary focus of all your thinking must be the reader. And Simon Dicketts, the writer, obviously sees the world through his reader's eyes and understands how they feel. Here, he is writing to the ordinary Callum or Kylie who doesn't quite belong in the 'achingly cool technology hall of London's most happening department store' (otherwise known as Selfridges).

Nor are they of the same ilk as the 'sound and vision technologist in the Marc Jacobs sandals'. But they do have the last laugh at such pretentiousness. Because, having checked out the kit they want to buy, they aren't daft enough to pay top price. No, they get it at a discount from Dixons.

When sex sells

That Dixons headline is a good example of how to lead the reader down one path, only to switch direction at the last second and leave them in a totally different place.

This subversion of expectation is one of the most powerful storytelling techniques. Remember Bruce Willis in *The Sixth Sense*? That film was a tad sombre, so here's a more light-hearted example.

A comic (Les Dawson, I think it was) might say, 'I'm going to rip my wife's knickers off as soon as I get home,' thus presenting us with an alarming mental picture of domestic life *chez* Dawson. Only for him to pause, grimace, put his hand down the back of his trousers and say, 'They're bloody killing me.'

We quickly process the first sentence, find a schema and predict the story's outcome. But, as a result, we are mentally off balance when the punchline is delivered, and its impact is all the greater for it.

Here's another example of a headline that uses this technique. At first sight it looks like another foray into the murky realm of marital sex.

**This summer, kiss your wife in places
she's never been kissed before**

Now, that's a pretty abruptive headline, and we notice it because it plays on our most basic instinct: sex. But as we read on we realize that the ad is for Four Corners Travel, who are selling us their wide range of new destinations for the coming holiday season.

In working out that these are the new places you can kiss your wife, the reader uses his wits to reconcile the disparate elements and, in so doing, gets what Beryl McAlhone and David Stuart call 'a smile in the mind'.[13]

The fact that many couples see their fortnight away each year as a chance to catch up on long-deferred rumpy-pumpy adds extra meaning to the headline, and makes the ad doubly satisfying.

As I said above, its abruptive quality comes from the suggestion of sex. And it works because the sex is relevant to the story. Here's another good example I saw yesterday when I was browsing the Virgin website.

I won't explain the problem/solution. All I need to tell you about the target audience is that a) they are English, and b) their 'old brain' and its basic instincts are still very active.

The headline is advertising the world's most sinful city, Las Vegas; and this is what it says:

**Come to a place where
your accent is an aphrodisiac**

Great stuff.

Now this and the other headlines we've seen look simple enough. However, I'm sure most took hours of hard thinking to create.

Here's David Abbott, the author of *The Economist* poster we saw a few pages back: 'I might rework a headline fifty or sixty times to get the thought and balance exactly right. If I think there's an ad in there I nag at it until it comes out. I'm often surprised how quickly time passes when I'm doing this. I look up and discover that I've been fiddling with the words for three hours.'[14]

Fifty or sixty variations. And that's just one headline he'd have been noodling away at. There would undoubtedly have been many others.

If the greatest writer of his generation had to put the hours in, you will too.

Keep the proposition pinned above your desk

Start by pinning the proposition on the wall above your desk. Then keep checking that your headlines are communicating, dramatizing or demonstrating that thought.

This is vital, because even the best writers come up with headlines that look good but miss the mark. Take, for example, the current campaign for the *Metro*, the free paper that's a welcome source of the latest news for the UK's morning commuters.

Now, I am not a party to the research they must have done. However, I'll hazard a guess that the proposition revolves around the social currency it gives us – i.e. a quick read of the *Metro* allows us to start and join in conversations with people when we get in to work.

And that is cleverly conveyed by the following headline, which was set out across the entire front page of the paper itself:

> **This METRO has no photos**
> **of your friend's beach**
> **holiday. Nor does it have**
> **alerts, notifications or**

**filtered photographs of
your cousin Gary's brunch.
It does, however, have
shedloads of news, sport,
showbiz, music, film and
comedy. The sort of stuff
you can actually like and
share in the real world.**

So far, so very good. But then you turn to the back page and see this headline:

**Whatever you do right
now, do NOT look up. That
enthusiastic foodie chap
from work is over there.
If he clocks you it'll be
spiralizer this and juicer
that, all the way to your
desk. Behind this METRO
is definitely the safest
place to be right now.
No doubt about it.**

It's a funny line. And, it's based on a problem we might have when travelling to work (most of us have ducked a colleague). But, it isn't *the* problem that the *Metro* solves. And therefore it isn't *the* reason why you would want to pick up the *Metro* in the morning. So I don't think it should be the subject of the advertising.

It's easy for me to be picky. And I know how difficult it is to deliver numerous executions in a big campaign. But when you're faced with that kind of brief, try to stay focused on your proposition, no matter how tempting it is to explore other avenues.

Let your subconscious do the work for you

Whether you're working on a big campaign or a one-off web page, make sure you have read and re-read the brief. This immersion in the background is vital.

Then write your headlines down on a pad. When you come up with one that's OK, put a circle round it. If you are working on a screen, put it in bold. Then move on and do some more.

The lines will come thick and fast at the beginning, but then, after a day or so, you'll dry up.

Don't worry, this is normal. You've simply got rid of your first thoughts, the ideas you've seen before and the clichés that are associated with the topic in question.

At which point, stop working on the headline and concentrate on something else. But have your notepad ready, and jot down the good ideas when they start popping into your head.

This game of patience was introduced by American adman James Webb Young in his book *A Technique for Generating Ideas* back in 1940. Some sixty-four years later, professor of psychology Arne Dietrich explained how it happens in his paper 'The Cognitive Neuroscience of Creativity'.

He classified Young's process as 'spontaneous and cognitive creativity' and traced its beginnings to the brain's prefrontal cortex. In the early stages, the prefrontal cortex focuses your attention while you're mulling over the details of the brief. At the same time, it relates those details to the stuff that's already in your head and acts as a 'search engine that "pulls" task relevant information from long term storage'.[15]

After you've got the predictable ideas out of your system and stopped working on the brief, your basal ganglia take over. But not that you'd know about it. No, they're operating in your subconscious while you're thinking about other jobs, going to the cinema, drinking with friends, watching football or fast asleep.

The basal ganglia hang out in the brain's Deep Web. Free from the constraints of consciousness, they play with the information, put together much looser combinations and produce fresher ideas. As Dietrich says, 'because there is no apparent effort or intention associated with these intuitive insights, they are often described as mysterious and indicated by such metaphors as "being hit by bricks" or the proverbial light bulb turning on.'[16]

Most people involved in creative pursuits rely on the subconscious. Loath as I am to use him as an example, Sir Paul McCartney famously knocked off 'Yesterday' one morning after having dreamed the entire tune.

I have never dreamed an advertisement, but I used to get a lot of ideas on the train home when I'd 'turned off' and was relaxing with the *Evening Standard*. As such, many a headline started life scribbled above the masthead, with numerous variations down the margins.

If nothing had come by the time I got to Beckenham Junction, that was OK. I was pretty sure that, given enough time, something would turn up.

Moreover, I also knew what to do if my deadline arrived before the basal ganglia had been able to work their magic.

What to do when you're stuck

You can start by writing 'How to . . .' plus the benefit you are offering.

It's a good idea. Just look at the title of this book. Pan Macmillan, the publisher, is clear about its subject. And anyone who wants to improve their commercial writing skills knows it's aimed at them.

Let's see how 'How to . . .' works using the examples we looked at earlier:

How to make money while others are losing theirs
(M&G Investments)

How to get to the top faster than your peers
(*The Economist*)

How to conquer your shyness and speak English with confidence (Wall Street English)

How to survive hell on earth (Musée de la Grande Guerre)

How to get the latest plasma TV at a fraction of the price others will pay (Dixons)

But 'How to . . .' is just one way to get your prospect's attention. If that doesn't help, then you can always write yourself a BuzzFeed headline.

2 ways to come up with a BuzzFeed headline

BuzzFeed was founded in 2007. Today, many observers see it as the future of digital journalism. Its rapid growth is largely down to its use of 'listicles', or lists and articles.

Have a look now at '29 things you need to know about blah blah' and '18 nasty things celebrities are saying about whatshisname'.

BuzzFeed's boffins know these work. For example, they've found out which numbers pull the best response. At the moment, it is '29 things'. Indeed, they are ruthless in their analysis, employing an in-house team of data scientists and an internal leadership board which ranks writers by the number of views they get.

Given their obsession with effectiveness, you'd be wise to learn BuzzFeed's lessons and write your headlines their way. Let's see how it'd work for the examples we've used thus far:

3 signs that say it's the right time to invest
  (M&G Investments)

7 business insights that will put you in pole position
  (*The Economist*)

5 ways to conquer your shyness about speaking English (Wall Street English)

9 ways to kill a man with the 20-inch French 'Rosalie' bayonet (Musée de la Grande Guerre)

4 ways to save money on your next plasma TV (Dixons)

These two techniques, 'How to . . .' and '3 ways to . . .'

can be used for press ads, subject lines, brochures, landing pages, inserts, banners, doordrops, you name it. Here, for example, is how they currently feature in *The Journal*, which is the blog on the excellent Mr Porter menswear site.

You have: 'How to find a perfect gift', 'How to look good in sweats', 'How to talk to a tailor', 'How to be as cool as James Bond', 'How to stay stylish and warm at any altitude', 'How to iron a shirt', 'Nine ways to master a black tie', 'Five art cities to visit right now', 'Six ways to look good at an art show' and 'Five ways to make a tux your own'.

Ask a question

Back to BuzzFeed and, when they aren't attracting readers with their listicles, they're doing so with quizzes. For example, they recently asked people to vote on whether a woman's dress was white and gold or black and blue. The article got 38 million views.

See if you can do something similar. It might not be a quiz. Just asking a question can be effective. For example:

Yes? No? Maybe? Is this the right time to make a killing on the stock market? (M&G Investments)

Answer these questions to see if you are ready for a place on the board (*The Economist*)

Are these the things that are stopping you speaking English? (Wall Street English)

How would you like your rat tonight: Fried? Sauteed? Raw? (Musée de la Grande Guerre)

How much would you like to save off the latest plasma TV: £50 . . . £80 . . . £115? (Dixons)

Focus on the problem

'Bad Back?' is one of the most effective headlines ever written. Why? Because one in three of us will, at some time, answer 'yes'. Which means this headline has spoken directly to tens of millions of us over the years.

When you are stuck for a headline, do something similar. Go back to the brief and the problem that the prospect is experiencing, and feature it in your headline. For example:

Worried about whether to stay in the market – or get out? (M&G Investments)

Scared that your colleagues know more than you do? (*The Economist*)

Are you too shy to try to speak English? (Wall Street English)

Do you have two hours to kill in Meaux this afternoon? (Musée de la Grande Guerre)

Can't afford that plasma TV you really want? (Dixons)

Put a quotation in your headline

When you quote someone else saying good things about your product or service, it's called a testimonial. And we'll be reading more about them when we cover body copy in the next chapter.

But you can also use a testimonial as your headline.

Often, you see existing customers being quoted in this way. But just reproducing some positive feedback from 'Mr Smith of Brighton' isn't convincing. Indeed, unless you provide more detail about 'Mr Smith of Brighton', it looks bogus. And that's the last impression you want to give about your company.

It is better to use someone who is regarded as an authority on the category in which you're operating. You might use a review from a respected blogger, a quote from a popular forum, a magazine or newspaper.

I saw a very good example in today's *Daily Telegraph*. It is for Newsworks, which does the marketing for the UK's national newspapers. The aim of the current campaign is to persuade advertisers to buy space in their publications.

So they've run this headline:

> **There's really strong evidence**
> **that engagement with traditional**
> **print is greater than engagement**
> **with so-called *new* media**

That's useful news if you're deciding where to spend your ad budget. And it is made more impressive by its source. They are the words of Sir Martin Sorrell, CEO of WPP, the biggest advertising holding company in the world.

Sir Martin is often derided by advertising's creative luvvies because of his business acumen. Yet, for exactly that reason, he is respected by the hard-headed business folk on the client side. And they are the target audience for this ad.

So the use of Sir Martin as the voice of authority is excellent. And his quote may well have got the response: 'That's interesting, tell me more.' But, in this case, there is no 'more'. Instead of demonstrating Sir Martin's point by running copy that engages and persuades the reader, the ad ends right there.

There isn't even a URL. So the people who are intrigued by this headline have nowhere to go to find out about Sir Martin's claim – or Newsworks' sales pitch.

It's a shame because the ad's authors have given us a good example of how to use a testimonial in a headline.

They have also, inadvertently, led us nicely to the next step in the process of writing better copy: what to say after you've done your headline.

Have you thought of having a subhead under your headline?

Once you've written your headline and grabbed your reader's attention, you then have to turn that attention into interest.

To do that, you must make it as easy as possible for the reader to move from headline to body copy. To help you, I'd like to recommend a technique that is unfashionable nowadays: the subhead under the headline.

Not so long ago, it was normal to follow your headline with a subhead, which served as a bridge to the body copy. But today's advertising minimalists pooh-pooh such tactics. As I said earlier, they are convinced that the best ad is the one that's been stripped of copy, subheads and even headlines.

Don't let them put you off. Take your lead from the excellent BBC News website. Its editors always follow their headlines with a subhead to make sure the reader knows what the copy beneath is about and where the story is heading.

It's the same with the world's most popular magazines. Their sub-editors realize that, even though their readers have bought the magazine for the articles, they still need help getting into the body copy.

The Economist's subscribers, who can scan a word in 300 milliseconds, are helped along by a subhead beneath the headline. Even an uber-cool magazine like *Wallpaper* follows this convention.

So, too, do the trashy downmarket gossip rag *Closer* and the trashy upmarket gossip rag *Tatler*. Which goes to show that, when it comes to needing a courteous helping hand down from the headline and into the copy, then Kipling was right: 'the Colonel's lady and Judy O'Grady are sisters under the skin'.

Why readers like you to be predictable

What I've said applies not only to press ads. You can use a subhead under your headline in web copy, a blog, brochure copy, emails and direct mail. They also help when you are writing internal documents to your colleagues, clients or suppliers.

That's because they provide information that helps the reader work out where the story is heading.

And the easier it is for them to tell where the story is heading, the more likely they are to read on.

Hree's an eamxlpe of tihs in atcoin. Wihle msot of tehse wrdos aeappr to be gbobydeloogk, you are albe to udnertsnad tehm bcesaue you arelady konw the sbucejt I'm wtirnig aobut.

As Ssaun Wienschnek elpxnias in *100 Tihgns Erevy Degsnier Ndees to Konw Abuot Ppleoe*: 'When you read you don't absorb exact letters and words and then interpret them later. You anticipate what will come next. The more previous knowledge you have, the easier it is to anticipate and interpret.'[17]

Or, as Yellowlees Douglas has it: 'Guessing what comes next is actually the mechanism that propels reading along, enabling us to interpret and comprehend what we read. Once we know the context of an article or novel, we can begin weighing everything we read.'[18]

The weighing of your work begins with the individual words you have used. Have you chosen the ones that say what you mean, and does your reader know them instantly? In short, it's a test of your and their vocabulary.

After that, the reader gains understanding from the order in which your words appear. Or, as my English teacher used to call it, syntax.

All of this is crucial to making yourself understood. And we shall have a closer look when we get into the body copy in Chapter 7. However, at this point, you probably have another more pressing problem.

How the hell do you get started?

6:

HOW TO WRITE YOUR BODY COPY

When I was running my agency, I'd get annoyed when someone handed in a piece of work with the apologetic caveat, 'It won't be very good, I'm a rubbish writer.'

In response, I'd quote the Australian actress Coral Browne and say that on the evidence of our first drafts, none of us can 'write "fuck" on a dusty venetian blind'.

I told them that the initial attempt is always the hardest. And that the fun begins only with the revisions.

But as I write that now, it's of little consolation. For despite having done all the necessary preparation, writing this first draft is still the equivalent of bleeding from the forehead.

I must overcome the urge to dry the breakfast pots, send off my two-year-old travel insurance claim to HSBC, ring the dentist to check whether my next appointment is this Wednesday or next Wednesday, and sort into pairs two weeks' worth of washed socks that are gathering ominously, like Alfred Hitchcock's birds, atop the kitchen radiator.

In short, the sure-fire way of doing the things I've been putting off for ages is to sit down to write a first draft. But let's plough on, shall we?

Write quickly

Staring at a blank screen *is* daunting. But don't let it get to you. Don't have a ritual that needs to be performed before you're ready to write. Don't wait for inspiration.

If you've done the preparation I described in Chapter 2 then you should be able to hit the keys running.

As David Abbott said, 'By the time I come to write, the structure of the argument is somehow in my brain. I spend a lot of time fact-finding and I don't start writing until I have too much to say.'[1]

All that fact-finding will stand you in good stead, too. For while you are doing your homework and building your structure, your subconscious will be working on the text. So let it take over. Don't revise as you work. Don't edit yourself.

And don't log out and start searching for more material. Or fret about it being good or bad. That carping voice will always be there. But don't worry: it hasn't singled you out for special criticism. Even the greatest writers hear it.

Just ask Stephen King: 'There's plenty of opportunity for self-doubt. If I write rapidly, putting down my story exactly as it comes into my mind, only looking back to check the names of my characters and the relevant parts of their back stories, I find I can keep up with my original enthusiasm and at the same time outrun the self-doubt that is always waiting to settle in.'[2]

Write as you speak

David Abbott and Stephen King advised you to just do it. But often you'll fail to get out of the blocks as quickly as you'd like. Indeed, you may pull up after the first five sentences.

So how does your writing keep its momentum?

Well, follow the advice of one of America's most respected copywriters, Jim Durfee, and 'don't "write" at all. Visualize the one person you want to influence, then sit that one person down across from you. Now talk to him or her through your pen, pencil, typewriter, word processor or whatever.'[3]

And, most importantly, write as you speak when you are concentrating hard on the conversation you are having. Simply begin your copy as if you were opening that conversation. That'll give you a flying start.

It certainly works for Jeremy Bernstein, the Group Creative Director at Deutsch New York. 'We have a mantra: "human spoken here". That basically means, speak in a way that people speak, that's conversational and colloquial – still well-written, but accessible to whoever your audience is. If your audience is very sophisticated, the language should be very sophisticated, but not complicated. People are people and like things that are easy to understand and smart.'[4]

Try writing to Warren Buffett's sisters

I'm not urging you to use the slang or profanities that add colour and emphasis to your everyday speech. Nor should you be inappropriately chatty.

What I mean is this: suppose you're face to face with

your bank manager asking for a second mortgage. You'd speak as you normally do, but with the correctness that the situation demands, wouldn't you?

Well, if you are writing to her, then that's the tone of voice you should adopt. Likewise, when you're addressing any serious subject, write as you would speak about it.

Handling billions of dollars of investors' savings is as serious as it gets. And writing to them is no laughing matter. Especially when you're telling them about the small fortune they now have invested – as opposed to the big one they started with.

It's a message Warren Buffett has had to deliver on occasion. Yet the world's most famous fund manager never lets gravity get in the way of clarity.

Here's his advice: 'Write with a specific person in mind. When writing Berkshire Hathaway's annual report, I pretend that I am talking to my sisters. I have no trouble picturing them: though highly intelligent, they are not experts in accounting or finance. They will understand plain English, but jargon may puzzle them. My goal is simply to give them the information I would wish them to supply me if our positions were reversed. To succeed, I don't need to be Shakespeare; I must, though, have a sincere desire to inform. No siblings to write to? Borrow mine: Just begin with "Dear Doris and Bertie".'[5]

Cut out the business verbiage

In financial services and the legal profession in particular, there are still those who are uncomfortable with this conversational style. They see it as unprofessional.

Peter Vierod, the founding partner at the Australian agency Friendly Persuasion, has heard this argument from many of his clients. As he told me, they often ask him: "'If you're a leader in your field, your writing should have a gravitas that befits its status, shouldn't it?" Another objection we hear is that by writing in a more straightforward way, you're somehow dumbing down a topic. Writing that is clear, simple and personable leaves the author naked with their thoughts in full view. This can feel uncomfortable for people who are used to cloaking their prose in the glad rags of business verbiage.'[6]

However, Peter has shown that, by stripping away such old-fashioned pretensions, you rid yourself of the unnatural affectations that make Business English so sterile. Better still, you automatically get on your reader's wavelength.

You've already started to tune in because your headline has grabbed their attention. Now your first paragraph must track from that headline (and subhead if you have one) and turn that attention into interest.

Make your first paragraph track from your headline

This may sound simple, but you'll see many first paragraphs that go off at a totally different tack to the idea in the headline.

I saw this recently in a full-page colour press advertisement. The headline says: 'The company that started Silicon Valley is making history again.'

Curiosity-arousing headlines don't come much better. That claim about starting Silicon Valley is interesting, and prompts the questions: 'Whaddya mean, *you* started Silicon Valley, is that true? What are you talking about?'

And I expected those questions to be nailed in the first paragraph of copy. But instead there was this: 'History is being made right now. One company is being separated into two industry leaders – the largest business separation ever.'

At which point the intrigue of that headline was lost. And so was this reader's attention.

It's pretty typical. For you often have to search the body copy for any reference to the story being told in the headline. This is crazy. The headline has three purposes: 1) get the reader's attention, 2) tell them what the copy is about and 3) tempt them to read the first paragraph.

If the first paragraph doesn't track, then you've thrown away the advantage that the headline has gained you. And you may never get another chance to tell your story – or sell your product to that reader.

Start where the reader is

We've just seen the importance of making your story track from headline to first paragraph. And there's a simple way of doing this: go straight into the details of the message in your headline.

A lot of writers recommend this. But it can be dangerous.

If you go immediately into the benefit of the product, you might get ahead of yourself. By that I mean you are starting where you *want* the reader to be, as opposed to where the reader actually *is*.

As Professor Siegfried Vögele, the pioneer of eye-tracking readership research, concluded: 'We simply have to adjust our approach according to our reader's low level of willingness to concentrate on our advertising material.'[7]

And, in many cases, the reader hasn't yet related to the problem that your product or service is going to solve for them. In short, they are not yet engaged.

Back on page 5, I explained how to achieve this when I said, 'readers become engaged with what you have written when they can see themselves in the story you are telling'. If you still buy that idea, then let's look at how a master copywriter used to do it.

A lesson from the best-paid copywriter ever

Back in the 1980s and 1990s, there was an American writer called Bill Jayme who used to charge upwards of $100,000 per mailpack.

Usually he was writing letters aimed at persuading people to take out magazine subscriptions. Which means his success was easily measurable, and his clients knew whether he was worth his huge fee.

Most concluded that he was.

He started his letters by creating little dramas that featured the problem the magazine's contents would solve.

Let's take *Business Week* as an example. The problem/solution there revolved around the danger of making badly informed decisions in business and about personal finances. The information provided by *Business Week* removed that danger.

So Bill Jayme started by asking, 'Hasn't it ever happened to you in business? It sure used to happen to me.' Then he described three scenarios in which you, the reader, might mess up because you don't have the necessary facts and analyses.

Only after a page of this scene-setting did Jayme reveal the solution: a subscription to *Business Week*.

And only then did he go into detail about how *Business Week* delivered its benefits.

Another example of starting where the reader is

Suppose you're selling a new stronger line of Finish dishwasher detergent to people who own such gadgets. Knowing that people are interested in new things, you could start your copy like this:

> Dear [name of person],
> I'd like to tell you about new Finish Extra.
> It's the first dishwasher detergent to cut through
> all those stubborn dried-on egg and pasta stains
> that your dishwasher cannot shift.

This is OK because it capitalizes on the newness of the product and goes straight to the benefit the user will enjoy. But it starts where the writer *wants* the reader to be – at a moment when the reader is not yet fully engaged with the problem/solution story.

As we've noted, the best way to get people engaged is to work them into that story. So, here's another opening:

> Dear [name of person],
> Do you know anyone who prefers to wash their

dishes by hand rather then pop them in their
dishwasher? I don't.

But have you noticed how some dried-on stains,
like egg and pasta, never come clean, so you end
up having to wash them by hand after all?

Well, that's why I'd like to tell you about new
Finish Extra. It's the first dishwasher detergent
to cut through all those stubborn stains your
dishwasher doesn't shift.

And another

I saw this one in the *Straits Times* when I was last in Singapore. It's for The Learning Lab, the leading enrichment
school in a country obsessed with educational excellence.

The ad was celebrating The Learning Lab's fifteenth
anniversary (a long time in a country just fifty-three years
old).

Usually such milestones are an occasion for much
corporate chest-beating. Not in this case, though. From the
headline, it's very clear who the focus of the ad is:

**The first thing we teach your child
is a love of learning**

The opening paragraphs home in even closer on the
parent/prospect:

If you have children, you'll want them to get the
very best from their education. Indeed, you're
probably one of the 7 in 10 Singaporeans who send
their youngsters to private tuition.

If so, you'll have realized a basic fact about the success and failure of those lessons: Drumming facts into your child's head does not work. It's a waste of your money and the child's time.

When your child is bored or unhappy in class, no amount of expensive tuition will help them. That's something we realized back in 2001. So, we created a new kind of lesson.

In running that copy, The Learning Lab has also given *us* a lesson in how to see the world – and the problem – through the eyes of the reader.

Some excellent opening paragraphs

The examples I've just given you come from email/direct mail and press. But starting where the reader is also applies to pretty much everything you write.

Here are five opening paragraphs to articles from the Christmas edition of *Trader Joe's Fearless Flyer*. The *Fearless Flyer* is the monthly newsletter of everybody's favourite US retailer. Indeed, for thirty years, it has been the supermarket chain's primary form of advertising.

Headline: 'Bacon-Wrapped Dates with Goat's Cheese'.
Body copy: 'You're planning a holiday party. You're thinking hors d'oeuvres, a few creative cocktails, and a good selection of wine. Nothing too fancy or complicated. You don't really have time to prep lots of little things for folks to eat. And yet, you'd like the food to be interesting, conversation-worthy, and most importantly, delicious. Where do you turn?'

Headline: 'Organic Triple Ginger Instant Oatmeal'.
Body copy: 'When the weather gives you a chill, there's nothing like hot cereal to warm you from the inside out, giving you the strength you need for the day ahead.'

Headline: 'Chocolate Marbles'.
Body copy: 'If you take a glance at Trader Joe's Chocolate Marbles, you'll be surprised that they're chocolate. You'll find yourself marvelling at how meticulously perfect they appear, how really round they are, how surprisingly shiny their finish. Your curiosity will no doubt get the better of you, and you'll definitely want to take a bite, just to be entirely sure they really are chocolate. And you'll find that, oh yes, this *is* chocolate.'

Headline: 'Peppermint Joe-Joe's Ice Cream'.
Body copy: 'You may be wondering why on earth we're advertising ice cream in December. You may think we've lost it.'

Headline: 'European Cookie Collection'.
Body copy: 'Is this a new product, you ask? Definitely not. But why don't I recognize the name, you ask? While we can't be sure (we're not inside your head, after all) we'll make a guess that you've seen these cookies in Decembers past . . .'

The folks who write the *Fearless Flyer* may *not* be inside the reader's head, but they try hard to understand what she's thinking as she's reading the copy.

Then they aim to get her head nodding. And these first few sentences achieve that. Like all good openings, they start with the reader's favourite subject. No, not the store's Peppermint Ice Cream or Chocolate Marbles. The reader's favourite subject is the reader, i.e. the 'you' that is referred to throughout.

This is as good an example of branded content as you'll find. Of course, the cult-like following that Trader Joe's has attracted don't use such highfalutin terms. They just see the *Fearless Flyer* as a quirky newsletter that views the store through their eyes and helps them make the right choices.

Simple stuff, brilliantly done.

Use your own experience to understand their emotional needs

When it *is* done brilliantly, seeing the world through your reader's eyes blossoms into empathy. This most fundamental of human qualities allows you to understand how the reader feels, recognize their emotional needs and adjust your story accordingly.

Obviously it requires a certain worldliness on the part of the writer. You've got to have been round the block a few times yourself before you can comfortably fit your aching feet into other people's shoes.

For my part, I didn't start as a writer until I was thirty years old and had held numerous mostly menial jobs that had nothing to do with marketing. Having said that, those jobs gave me a better preparation for writing copy than my twenty-three-year-old colleagues got from advertising college. For they knew a lot about advertising, but very little about life as it was led by the folks we were advertising to.

Apparently, such experience is also vital to the writer of fiction. Here's novelist Joanna Trollope speaking at the 2015 Emirates Festival of Literature:

In order to write good fiction you need to have got a lot of living under your belt. And that includes the pain as well as the joy. It's rather an unkind thing to have to say and I don't mean it unkindly, but I always say to people 'you will write much better fiction after the age of thirty-five than before. Merely because life will have knocked you about a bit by then.'

You have to be in tune with other people; you have to understand that the suffering of other people is not negligible then, even if you think they are making the most enormous fuss . . . What I try to do is get inside head after head after head.[8]

Win your reader over with empathy

As Trollope implies, in fiction, success comes when the writer takes all they know about human nature and creates a main character with whom the reader can empathize.

However, as we saw on page 24, when you are writing commercial copy, the hero of the story is the reader, and it is the writer's job to imagine what it is like to be them.

As you may have worked out already, such empathy is necessary throughout the whole writing process.

To begin with, you need empathy to do the problem/solution dynamic properly. Without it, you'll never understand why the prospect might want the product or service you are selling.

Then you have to be able to empathize with your reader's reaction to the constant din of marketing communications. And make sure you only write headlines that tell them something useful.

After that, there's the first paragraph that lets them know you are in tune with them. If you are starting with their problem, you must show you know how they feel.

Then, as you begin to reveal the solution to the reader, use empathy to build a rapport with them. Here are a few examples:

'I know it's frustrating for you. You're paid to do the IT strategy in your company but you have to spend most of your day down in the server room doing all the grunt jobs.'

'Having said that, I realize you may never have heard of us, and you'll be wondering if we can be trusted.'

'When you're being briefed on a job, do you exude confidence and assure everyone "everything will be fine", only to go "Agh!" as soon as they've left the room?'

'By now you may be thinking, "I'd find that useful but how do I convince my Finance Director to pay for it?"'

'The only thing better than getting a great deal on your holiday is knowing that the person sitting next to you on the plane paid twice as much.'

'You and I know we're not the cheapest on the market. In fact, we're pretty expensive. But . . .'

'Do you no longer glance back at your car once you've locked the door and started to walk away?'

As you'll notice from a couple of these examples, using empathy is a good way of showing that you understand the reader's doubts about buying what you are selling.

Back on page 47, I advised you to factor in your reader's resistance when you are structuring your message. Once you've done that, showing a bit of empathy is a good way of acknowledging and then overcoming that resistance.

A touch of empathy also makes your writing more engaging, because if you relate to the reader then she will relate to you. And this rapport will differentiate your messages from those visitations from the alien world of marketing sent to her by your rivals.

She may even get to like you. Which is your ultimate goal. For, as the great English copywriter Tony Brignull said, 'A state of friendliness is best between buyer and seller.'[9]

Give them the facts

If you win your way into the reader's heart with empathy, then you get into their head with facts. And you should start dropping these in somewhere just south of your headline and your opening paragraphs.

The former gets the reader's attention. The latter gets them interested by relating the headline's promise to their experience.

It may take another paragraph or two to strengthen the reader's interest. But then, to turn that interest into desire, you'll need the hard facts that back up the claims you've made.

If you look back at the brief, you'll find these facts in the section under question 7.

For example, suppose you've said that your copier–printer is the fastest on the market. Don't merely tell your reader how many copies it zips through per minute. That figure means little to them unless you put it in context.

So make it real by working out how the increased speed of output affects your prospect's working life. Maybe you can say that a week's normal printing can now be done in four and a half days. Which, in effect, gives them Friday afternoon off.

In other words, appeal to their self-interest.

Then pile in with the facts that back that up. Quote any comparative tests that have pitched your copier–printer against others on the market. If those tests have been run by someone else, great. If not, stage your own. Then have them certified by a respected third party.

If your copier–printer has won awards from industry bodies for its speed of output, mention them. Likewise quote the trade press or other authoritative writers who have commented on how fast it is.

But if you do use endorsements from trade bodies, magazines or bloggers, it helps if your reader has heard of them. To be on the safe side, give a little explanation as to how important your sources are. This makes their endorsement even more impressive.

If there's a new technology behind your super-fast copier–printer, then briefly explain how this breakthrough works. (Remember, readers like to get news.) If it is the result of the $750 million your company spends each year on research and development, mention this fact and quote that figure.

In business-to-business copy such as this, it is vital that you support your promise with as much information as possible. That's because your reader will probably have to argue on your behalf to get funding for the purchase – so the more facts you give them, the more chance they have of getting the money.

Then again, consumers can be just as hard-nosed. After all, it's *their* money they are spending, so you've got to be even more convincing.

If, for instance, you're claiming that your English language school has the best teaching method, then cite the percentage of your students who graduate each year. Then get hold of competitive figures, and compare yours with those of rival schools.

Moreover, if your method has been endorsed by a major teaching institution like Harvard or Cambridge, mention that as well.

If there's a reason why you achieve such excellence, explain it. It could be that you only have four pupils per class, so teachers can give personal guidance to each student. It may be that your one-on-one online lessons replicate the learning process we all experience as infants when mastering our mother tongue. Get these facts down.

Finally, a money-back guarantee for all students who don't graduate is a great way of backing up your promise. If you're willing to make the only such guarantee in the market, the reader will be reassured that your method really must be the best.

When facts aren't enough

If you've actually invented a better mousetrap – and proved it with facts that support your claim – you can rightly expect customers to beat a path to your door.

But maybe it's not that simple.

As Rory Sutherland, the UK ad industry's expert on behavioural economics and an excellent copywriter himself, points out, marketing has an important secondary role: reducing customers' levels of anxiety surrounding the purchase. As Rory explains, 'We seem to be very, very nervy people, so one of the first roles of marketing is to foster reassurance that what we're doing isn't weird and doesn't stand out.'[10]

In other words, you have to let people know they are not risking financial loss by investing in your new-fangled trap. Moreover, they're not going to be laughed at when the neighbours pop in and catch sight of it.

Such sensitivity was recognized thirty years ago by Siegfried Vögele in his research into what he called 'the dominating questions' prospects asked when reading copy. After those driven by self-interest came a series of questions that were always asked, regardless of target group or product for sale: 'Who has bought this before me?', 'Is it really the right one for me?', 'What would my boss say?', 'What would my family think?' and 'What would my friends and neighbours say?'[11]

The easiest way of removing such anxiety is to tell the reader that people like them have already bought the thing, and they're enjoying using it.

Use testimonials

If you are writing to people who could be regarded as 'early adopters' or 'cool hunters', relax. You won't need testimonials because these trendsetters pride themselves on getting to new things first.

Likewise, testimonials aren't essential if you're selling the number one brand in a particular category. The fact that it *is* the number one brand reassures people that they aren't making an economic or social faux pas.

In most other cases, however, you'd be wise to use testimonials from satisfied users. I intimated why in the section above when I said that people are wary of standing out from the crowd. Apparently there's a neurological reason for this urge to conform.

In 2011 Jamil Zaki, a psychologist at Stanford University, and his colleagues found that the urge to 'groupthink' can be traced to 'the ventromedial prefrontal cortex, a part of the brain's reward centre that lights up when we encounter things we want, like a chocolate bar. Zaki's team found that it also activates when people are told what others think. And the more this part of the brain responds to information about group opinion, the more someone will adjust their opinion towards the consensus.'[12]

To foster groupthink, use quotations from satisfied customers.

Now I know such advice might seem old hat, but that's because testimonials have been given a bad name by this kind of thing:

'A truly professional service' – E. R. of Birmingham.

The quote is too bland to be persuasive, and the attribution is too vague to be believable. Instead, the testimonial should explain what it is that makes the service 'truly professional'. Then give the satisfied customer's name, and as much of their address as possible.

If you are writing business-to-business, get a testimonial from someone who works for a successful company operating in the reader's field. Then cite the person's name, job title and company.

In all cases, try to have the testimonial address the problem/solution dynamic that is driving your sales message. The reader is then reassured a) that they are not alone in facing that problem, b) of the efficacy of your claim and c) by the fact that others are already benefiting from your product or service.

If you have lots of impressive testimonials, why limit yourself to one? Indeed, if you're writing for digital, the more the merrier. Just choose the one or two testimonials that you want to appear in your body copy. Then use a hyperlink to take your reader to a page featuring as many testimonials as they wish to read.

They'll probably just scan them. But the fact you have so many happy customers is proof you can deliver on your promise.

Similarly, if you're writing for a website, make sure the reader can scroll down to reviews and ratings left by your customers or clients. It doesn't matter if they are not experts. In fact, to many of your readers, social validation for their choice is strongest when it comes from ordinary consumers like themselves.

Susan Weinschenk cites one study that 'researched three kinds of rating and reviews at a bookstore website: reviews by regular visitors to a website, experts on the topic, and recommendations from the website itself. All three types influenced behaviour, but the reviews by regular visitors were the most influential.'[13]

Have a clear call to action

OK, you've got your reader's attention with a headline that promises them a benefit. You've got them interested by explaining how that promise solves a problem they are experiencing.

You've stimulated their desire by giving them the facts

about how you'll deliver on the promise. And you've convinced them this is a safe choice by showing them that their peers are already enjoying the benefits.

This means you've covered off the AIDC in AIDCA. And for that matter, you've done the problem and the solution in your three-act play.

Now all that's needed is the final act: the resolution which tells the reader how they can get the solution working for them.

I say 'all that's needed' as if it's an afterthought. However, it is anything but. And I mean that both figuratively and literally. For if you are writing for the web, tablet or mobile, the call to action should appear near the very top of your message as well as at its end.

That's because, unlike the case with offline media, the reader cannot see there's an opportunity to get in touch until they scroll down. So having a clickable link to a response mechanism up front will increase your response rates.

Either way, whether online or offline, be clear about what you want the reader to do and what's in it for them. If you want them to send for more information, tell them exactly what they'll be learning – and how they'll gain from that knowledge.

If, for example, you're offering a guide to playing the stock market, tell them they'll learn five key facts that have helped other investors make money. Or explain how they'll discover the seven mistakes that have cost other investors their savings.

If you want to arrange a meeting with them, don't wimp out with, 'I look forward to getting together with you.' Ask them 'Are you free for a coffee next Wednesday at 2.00?

I'll call you this afternoon to see if that's OK, or to set up another time that suits you better.'

And if you want them to buy from you, tell them how much your product costs. If you are charging less than the market leader, tell them the saving they'll make.

If you are putting up your prices on such and such a date, tell them that, too. And that they should order now to avoid the increase.

Inject urgency

Using a time-sensitive deadline like this prompts the reader to buy right now. And the reader needs all the coaxing you can give them. Quite simply, it is easier for them to think about it later . . . to ask their partner's opinion . . . to go to the pub and do it when they get back . . . tomorrow . . . at the weekend . . . never.

So think of a way to overcome their last-ditch resistance to parting with their cash.

There's an example of this every time you go on easyJet's site. You pop in the destination you're thinking of going to, and the dates. Then the price comes up along with a couple of prompts: '39 people looking at this route' and 'last booked two minutes ago'.

So what starts as a casual visit to find ballpark costs on a flight to somewhere you're thinking of going suddenly becomes a lot more urgent. You tell your partner, 'Blimey, it's only £75. But with all these other people looking at the route, who knows what it'll cost next time we log on.'

And, fifteen minutes after going to easyJet just to browse the site, you've booked a weekend away.

You're under even more pressure when you go to Expedia.com. Because once you've found a price you like, you get the equivalent of a 'last call' when you're told there are 'only two seats left at this price'.

And if you resist that, log off and then revisit a little later, you're greeted with a message like this: 'Flight prices to [name of your destination] on December 2nd–7th are likely to rise 18% in the next 5 days.'

Try to introduce a similar kind of prompt in your call to action. If you are selling a seminar to your customers, explain there are only 210 places available, and that last time you held this event you sold out within forty-eight hours.

You could then tell your customer that, because of your relationship, you have reserved a place for them for twenty-four hours. And thereafter, send them a text or an email letting them know how many tickets have gone thus far.

Scarcity is a great driver. Especially if your reader is tempted to buy something and then finds it's in limited supply.

So, if you're offering a Two-Year Fixed Interest Cash Bond, tell your reader there's a limit to how much money you can take in from investors. And, that once that limit is reached, the bond is closed. Then explain the vast amount of money that's already been invested, and say that you expect to reach that limit on such-and-such a date.

This helps speed the sale in a couple of ways: it tells the reader to act now or miss out. And it takes away their fear of social and financial embarrassment by letting them know that a lot of other people think this is a good deal.

Make them an offer – preferably free

When you write your call to action, bear this in mind: your reader likes to make a killing. For instance, in the UK about 40 per cent of our food shopping is bought to take advantage of a promotion of some kind.[14] And, very often, the type of product that ends up in the shopping basket wasn't even on the original shopping list.

Clearly, incentives work. So if you plan to give your reader a discount or make some other offer, then here's where you tell them. Good sales execs often hold back such deals for the close of the argument. They know they help overcome their client's final resistance.

In your case, make sure the reader notices your offer by putting it in a subhead like the one above. And instil a sense of urgency by being clear about the closing date for the offer.

You may not want to give money off. Indeed, discounting can reflect badly on the quality, efficacy or popularity of the product or service you're selling.

However, you can still offer them something to get them to reply immediately. It could be a report on the sector your reader works in. It could be a free travel guide, if you're selling holiday services. Whatever it is, if it is 'free', don't be bashful. Use that word in your subhead.

Then tell them exactly how to get in touch with you. If you want them to buy from you online, allow them to click a link to your order form. If you want them to phone you, give them your number and the hours your lines are open – and if it's a free call, tell them. If you want them to visit your store, give them your opening hours, a link to a map plus the address details they'll need to get clear directions from their satnav.

Put them in the driver's seat

They may prefer to get in their cars, visit your store and handle the merchandise rather than go online. If that's the case, it's a good job you've offered them that option.

In fact, giving them a choice can have a big impact on the response you get. As Rory Sutherland, vice-chairman of Ogilvy Group UK, suggests, 'The medium of engagement is often far more important than what might conventionally be called the "core product offering". I first noticed this in my very early days as a direct marketer – we learned that allowing people to respond to a letter by telephone or by post, rather than by insisting on one or the other, massively increased response to any [American Express] mailing. Logically it seemed strange: either you want an American Express Card or you don't – surely the option to request one by telephone should not make much difference.'[15]

But it does. And you should let your reader choose the way of responding.

And finally, when possible, take away the last element of doubt they might have by offering them a guarantee of satisfaction. We've seen how they fear making a choice that leaves them financially or socially embarrassed. This gives them the reassurance of knowing they can get their money back, and save face, too.

And on that happy note, your three-act story of problem, solution and resolution has been told.

So push your copy aside for twenty-four hours, grab a large glass and open a bottle of wine. You've earned it, because getting to the end of your first draft of copy is the hardest part of any writing you'll do.

Cheers.

7:

YOUR SECOND DRAFT: PUT THESE THINGS IN

I hope you didn't overdo it on the vino. If you did, then reconcile yourself to this: your first draft will be as rough as you feel.

But don't despair, everybody's is. As the world's greatest lyricist, Stephen Sondheim, says: 'a musical isn't written, it is rewritten.'[1]

Both you and your copy will recover. Your first draft is the raw young wine which, with due care and enough time, will become your bottle of Château Lafite-Rothschild.

So let's start by putting your hangover to good use. Imagine you are the reader: thick-headed, irritable, distracted.

Then ask yourself:

Will my headline grab this person's attention?

Have I shown that I understand their problem / point of view?

Have I been clear about the solution / alternative point of view?

Have I given them proof that I can back up my promise?

Have I anticipated their doubts and overcome them?

Have I told them exactly what I want them to do?

If not, get out your brief and your copy structure, and start to rework your copy.

If, on the other hand, you've got all the elements in

roughly the right order, then congratulations. After the pressure of the blank screen and the first draft, the next bit should be fun.

Have you broken the copy up with subheads?

Start by printing off your work and holding it up at arm's length. Will the reader know what it is about without reading the copy?

Probably not, if you are relying solely on the headline to give them their main clue. So, as Steve Krug explains in his masterful book on web usability *Don't Make Me Think*: 'Use plenty of headings. Well-written, thoughtful headings interspersed in the text act as an informal outline or table of contents for a page. They tell you what each section is about or, if they're less literal, they intrigue you. Either way, they help you decide which parts to read, scan or skip. In general, you'll want to use more headings than you'd think and put more time into writing them.'[2]

On page 53 we saw that your headline and these subheads not only tell the reader what the story is about, they allow the reader to find a schema that prepares them for what's coming next.

Captions under pictures and illustrations serve the same purpose. You'll find that most newspapers and magazines pop a caption under their photographs for this very reason. Yet in advertising, we rarely use them. Stupid, eh?

Subheads are also useful if you have more than one benefit to communicate. They allow you to draw attention to the additional ways you can help the reader.

And your subheads give the reader an alternative point of entry into the body copy. If a particular subhead interests them more than the piece's headline, then that's where the reader will start.

Like Krug above, Jakob Nielsen, the expert on how to get read on the web, is a great fan of subheads. We'll look at his views on this and other ways you can use your layout to make things easier for the reader in Chapter 10.

But for now, let's get back to your first draft and start knocking it into shape.

Have you used the right words?

The right words are those that make your meaning clear. And the best are the ones we use all the time.

That's certainly what Stephen King recommends: 'Remember that the basic rule of vocabulary is *use the first word that comes to your mind, if it is appropriate and colorful*. If you hesitate and cogitate, you will come up with another word – of course you will, there's always another word – but it probably won't be as good as your first one, or as close to what you really mean.'[3]

Usually these words have an Anglo-Saxon root. You'll recognize them because, compared to those with a Greek or Latin root, they are short and refer to concrete objects or actions.

We use Anglo-Saxon words all the time, and without thinking. They just pop out of our mouths or ping up on our screens.

Historians Robert Lacey and Danny Danziger point out, 'Computer analysis of the English language as spoken today shows that the hundred most frequently used words are all of Anglo-Saxon origin . . . When Winston Churchill wanted to rally the nation in 1940, it was to Anglo-Saxon that he turned: "We will fight on the beaches; we shall fight on the landing grounds; we shall fight in the fields and the streets; we shall fight in the hills; we shall never surrender". All these stirring words came from Old English as spoken in the year 1000.'[4]

There was, however, one exception. Appropriately enough under the circumstances, the French import was 'surrender'.

If English isn't your first language, write in Anglo-Saxon

Anglo-Saxon words leave little room for ambiguity. Indeed, they force us to say exactly what we mean.

Even people who don't have English as a first tongue can benefit from their precision. For example, Haruki Murakami is one of Japan's most successful living novelists. But when he started out, he felt the same inhibitions and awkwardness that afflict all of us when we're trying to write an email or a document.

So one day, in desperation, he decided to write in English. Here's what he discovered: 'Needless to say, my ability in English composition didn't amount to much. My vocabulary was severely limited, as was my command of English syntax. I could only write simple, short sentences. Which meant that, however complex and numerous the thoughts running around my head might be, I couldn't even attempt to set them down as they came to me. The language had to be simple, my ideas expressed in an easy-to-understand way, the descriptions stripped of all extraneous fat, the form made compact and everything arranged to fit a container of limited size. The result was a rough, uncultivated kind of prose . . . To sum up, I learnt that there is no need for a lot of difficult words. I didn't have to try to impress people with beautiful turns of phrase.'[5]

We're not dumbing things down, we're making them clear

I am not arguing for dumbing down. But your hold on the reader's attention is so weak that you simply cannot afford to lose them by showing off your love of words or wordplay.

David Abbott was the most cerebral (or do I mean clever?) of advertising men, but when it came to writing ads he said, 'I am not interested in words. I don't own a thesaurus, I don't do crosswords and my dictionary has pictures in it. Words, for me, are the servants of the argument and on the whole I like them to be plain, simple and familiar.'[6]

Like I say, I'm not arguing for dumbing down. While you should opt for a common word over one that's obscure, the intellectual level at which you pitch your argument should always be determined by that of your audience.

For example, let's stick with David Abbott and his work for *The Economist*.

We mentioned on page 61 that the problem/solution revolved around *The Economist* giving its readers the business intelligence they needed to succeed. When Abbott approved the poster headline 'To err is human, to um, err is unforgivable', he assumed that the well-read people he was targeting would be familiar with Alexander Pope's adage, 'To err is human; to forgive, divine' and would get the joke – and the point.

There's no lowering of intellectual standards in that headline, is there?

Nor would anyone question the intellectual rigour that Warren Buffett brings to his role as chairman of Berkshire Hathaway. Yet as Ian Harris, associate creative director of communications agency Gatehouse, explains: 'If you study Warren Buffett's writing over fifty years, there's a correlation between success and simplicity. Basically, the richer he becomes the simpler his writing . . . The age you'd need to understand his writing falls from seventeen years old in 1974, to just twelve years old in 2013.'[7]

So what are the words you should be using?

Pick the words that have a commonly understood, fixed meaning. And use them instead of their more complex alternatives. For example:

> **about**, not **approximately**
> **best**, not **optimum**
> **cut out**, not **eliminate**
> **eat**, not **consume**
> **end**, not **terminate**
> **finish**, not **finalize**
> **get**, not **acquire** or **obtain**
> **help**, not **facilitate**
> **let**, not **permit**
> **limits**, not **parameters**

make, not **formulate**
see, not **envisage**
speed up, not **expedite**
spread, not **disseminate**
start, not **initiate**
take part, not **participate**
think, not **conceptualize**
– and, please, never the atrocious **ideate**

When you use words your reader might not fully understand, your copy loses clarity, and you risk losing your reader. Moreover, if you search the thesaurus for a less obvious word than initially springs to mind, you risk misusing the new one – and looking foolish. I've seen this a myriad of times.

For example, as in the last sentence; which should read, 'I've seen this myriad times.'

So keep things simple. In the list above, all the words on the left are short and, in most cases, immediately communicate an action that is being performed. Those on the right have more than one syllable and are more abstract.

Which neatly introduces us to our best friends in the fight to get and keep our reader's attention.

Choose active verbs instead of passive verbs

OK, I'll try to get down in two pages what it took my English teacher three terms to drum into my head. (Deep breath . . .)

Let's start with Stephen King: 'Two pages of the passive voice – just about any business document ever written, in other words, not to mention reams of bad fiction – make me want to scream. It's weak, it's circuitous and it's frequently tortuous as well.'[8]

What gets King so angry? Well, with a passive verb, the subject of the sentence ('I', 'you', 'he/she/it', 'we', 'you' or 'they') isn't doing anything.

For example, as regards this book: 'It is being written by me' is passive. And it's weak, because the subject – 'it' – isn't pushing things forward. It is letting things happen.

Conversely, with an active verb, the subject of the sentence is doing something. For example, 'I am writing it.'

Similarly, 'you are reading this page' is active. Because 'you', the subject, are doing something, i.e. 'reading'.

But 'the page is being read by you' is passive. Again, the subject, 'the page', is just a bystander in the sentence.

Moving on, 'I'll write 2,000 words this afternoon and then have some tea' is active, but 'Some tea will be had this afternoon when 2,000 words have been written' is passive.

If those 2,000 words are written in the passive sense, then it's unlikely you'll bother reading them.

That's because psycholinguists, psychologists, cognitive and educational psychologists agree with Stephen King. Indeed, they are convinced that readers struggle with the passive voice and understand us better when we use the active form.

First get the chronology right, and then the cause and effect

Not only do readers prefer the active voice. When they look at a sentence, they expect the order of events that you've described to be the order of events as it actually happened.

So 'I'll write 2,000 words this afternoon and then have some tea' helps them understand, because they can imagine me passing the 1,999 mark, pushing back my chair, getting up and making a cuppa.

Writing chronologically is the best way to get your reader to look at your squiggles and visualize what is happening. It also enables you to link actors to actions, and describe the dynamic of cause and effect.

By that I mean, if you do A, then as a result, B will happen. Or, to keep our conceit going, 'I'll write 2,000 words this afternoon [cause], then have some tea' [effect].

We saw cause and effect at work in our section on how to write a proposition. For example, 'Send us your old, broken or unwanted gold jewellery [cause] and you can have ready cash in your hand in less than 48 hours [effect].'

Or, 'When you start using our new software [cause], you can cut your Day Sales Outstanding by 25 per cent [effect].'

This imposes a pleasing order on events. Pleasing? Well, yes, we humans like to impose order on chaos. Indeed, we can't help it, for it's the way we think. As Susan Greenfield, professor of synaptic pharmacology at Oxford University, explains, 'When you think, you go through a sequence of steps where the order is all-important . . . it is linear, it is sequential. Thinking is movement, step by step by step by step confined to the brain.'[9]

And so, if you order your sentences properly, they'll be processed quickly.

If, however, you disrupt the chronology and write 'Some tea will be had this afternoon when 2,000 words have been written,' your reader has to get to the end and then reassemble the information before they make sense of it.

'Some tea . . . what?' is their brain's reaction. And not

simply because the chronology is out of whack and the causal relationship is vague. Another problem is caused by what your teacher used to call poor syntax.

Syntax, or how to arrange the subject, verb and object

As we've seen, understanding comes from the reader's ability to predict where the story is heading. And their brain finds it much easier to anticipate the action if the first thing it bumps into is a subject and an active verb.

Yellowlees Douglas sums it up this way, 'Unconsciously, readers begin comprehending sentences only after they reach the grammatical subject. Once they locate the subject, the comprehension process begins, resembling – let's say, for the sake of visualization – an intake of breath. After readers encounter the subject, they hold their virtual breath until they stumble across the verb, completing the main action, the core of any sentence.'[10]

Let's give 'I'll write 2,000 words this afternoon and then have some tea' one last airing. It works because 'I [subject] will write [verb] 2,000 words [object]' sets the scene and generates a momentum that carries the reader to the end of the sentence.

Along with the ability to a) recognize the words you've used and b) work out context through the appropriate schema, this syntactical processing is the third way that your reader makes sense of what you have written.

You see repeated subject/verb/object combinations (plus the deft use of cause and effect and the presentation of persuasive facts) in the example I'm about to show you.

Purists rightly point to its preponderance of passive verbs. But the ad is widely regarded as the most influential of all time, so perhaps we can cut its author, Julian Koenig, some slack.

He wrote it for Volkswagen, and its layout comprised a picture of the VW Beetle above the one-word headline: 'Lemon'.

This is a curiosity-arousing headline that has the same abruptive effect as David Abbott's 'I never read The Economist' line, which we saw on page 61. The reader is intrigued as to why the advertiser should be saying bad things about their product. And goes to the body copy to discover that:

This Volkswagen [subject] missed [verb] the boat [object].

The chrome strip on the glove compartment [subject] is blemished [verb] and must be replaced [verb]. Chances are you [subject] wouldn't have noticed [verb] it [object]; Inspector Kurt Kroner [subject] did [verb].

There are 3,389 men at our Wolfsburg factory with only one job [subject]: to inspect [verb] Volkswagens at each stage of production [object]. (3,000 Volkswagens [subject] are produced [verb] daily; there are more inspectors than cars.)

Every shock absorber [subject] is tested [verb] (spot checking won't do), every windshield [subject] is scanned [verb]. VWs [subject] have been rejected [verb] for surface scratches barely visible to the eye [object].

Final inspection [subject] is [verb] really something! VW inspectors [subject] run [verb] each car [object] off the line onto the Funktionsprüfstand (car test stand) [object]; tote up [verb] 189 check points [object], gun ahead [verb] to the automatic brake stand [object] and say [verb] 'no' to one VW out of fifty [object].

This preoccupation with detail [subject] means [verb] the VW [subject] lasts [verb] longer and requires [verb] less maintenance [object], by and large, than other cars. (It [subject] also means [verb] a used VW [subject] depreciates [verb] less than any other car [object].)

We [subject] pluck [verb] the lemons [object]; you [subject] get [verb] the plums [object].

That copy set the tone for what became the most successful press advertising campaign ever. Its style inspired a generation of writers. Yet for Bill Bernbach, the head of the agency that produced it, there was a simple secret to its power. He explained it in three words: 'subject, verb, object'.[11]

Don't plonk words in front of the subject

If understanding starts when the reader reaches the subject, don't slow her down by piling a lot of information in front of that subject. For example, 'Given the earlier problem with the WiFi, I'll write 2,000 words this afternoon and then have some tea.'

The same goes for words coming between the subject and the verb. Some experts believe you should avoid putting even one word in there, thus: 'I'll quickly write 2,000 words this afternoon and then have some tea.'

Stephen King is violently against this. Indeed, he'd kill me for inserting 'violently'. In his opinion, 'The adverb is not your friend. Adverbs, you will remember from your own version of Business English, are words that modify verbs, adjectives or other adverbs, They're the ones that usually end in -ly. Adverbs, like the passive voice, seem to have been created with the timid writer in mind.'[12]

And neither you nor I want to be timid writers, do we?

No, we want to come up with stirring copy like this passage of subject/verb/object combinations and good old Anglo-Saxon (and occasional Latin) words. They were written for Steve Jobs and describe the people he had in mind when he created the Apple Mac:

> Here's to the crazy ones. The misfits. The trouble-makers. The round pegs in the square holes. The ones who see things differently. They're not fond of rules. And they have no respect for the status quo. You can quote them, disagree with them, glorify or vilify them. About the only thing you can't do is ignore them. Because they change things. They push the human race forward. And while some may see them as the crazy ones, we see genius. Because the people who are crazy enough to think they can change the world, are the ones who do.

Steve Jobs didn't like adverbs either

Incidentally, when Steve Jobs was looking for a strapline to sum up what Apple was all about, someone suggested 'Think Differently'. But Jobs, like Stephen King, saw the energy-sapping weakness in modifying an active verb like 'think' with the adverb 'differently'.

Instead, he insisted on the less grammatically correct but

much more powerful 'Think Different', in which different is a noun, as in the equally inspirational 'Think Big'.

Going back to 'The Crazy Ones', it is the voice-over to a wonderful commercial that features black and white footage of such mavericks as Einstein, Amy Johnson, Bob Dylan, Maria Callas, Gandhi, Martin Luther King and Picasso.

I show this film when doing my occasional seminars on marketing and writing. And I assure you that nine out of ten people in the audience have a deep-down, never-to-be-admitted but absolutely undeniable inkling that this film is just a little bit about them. That's because it is a glorious celebration of the human spirit, and they empathize with, and see themselves in, its maverick personalities.

As I've said throughout, getting your audience to feel that they are in the story is key to putting your message across. Coming up next is a simple way to make that happen with everything you write.

Use the most powerful short word of them all: you

There's one short word that you should work into your copy as often as possible. It is 'you'.

In fact, when you are reading your first draft, check that 'you' appears three times more than 'I', 'we' or 'our'. If the latter predominate, then you've probably been banging on about how great you and your product are.

But if you have used 'you' in a higher ratio, then chances are you've been looking at the thing you're selling through the eyes of your reader.

This is good because it trains you to see not just the

product, but the whole scenario in which your message is being delivered, from your reader's point of view.

And that in turn enables you to realize that, as far as they're concerned, they are not the 'reader'. Nor do they see themselves as the 'audience', the 'consumer', the 'customer', the 'target', the 'user', the 'browser', the 'punter' or the 'prospect'.

They are the heroes of their own stories. Selfie-stick extended. Camera slightly higher than the face. Head tilted to one side. Ready for their close-up.

You, on the other hand, are playing the tiniest of uncredited bit parts in their drama. Indeed, you weren't supposed to have been allocated a line, and yet here you are photobombing their shot, and trying to steal, if not a scene, then a minute of their time.

As we said from the start, if you're going grab to their attention for a minute then make sure that they are the hero of your story, too.

This is useful for clients to remember. For them, the individual they're aiming their ads at often exists only as .000001 per cent of a piece in a PowerPoint pie chart.

In agencies, it can be worse. Creatives, if they consider the customer at all, are often dismissive. Indeed, you can trace this snide attitude back to the 'glory days' of British advertising. Then, the standard packaged goods commercial aimed at housewives was known as '2Cs in a K'. If I tell you that 'K' stands for kitchen, you'll figure out the rest for yourself, and conclude that the biggest 'Cs' actually worked in the agencies.

Here's an example of the power of 'you'

This was a letter sent to American Express Green Card-members, aimed at getting them to move up to the more expensive Gold Card. These people had been Cardmembers for several years yet neither had they applied for the Gold Card, nor had Amex invited them to join.

Had Amex done so, then they'd have simply explained to the Green Cardmember all the extra benefits they'd enjoy by trading up to the Gold Card. But this letter took a different tack.

Dear [Name],

I am writing to invite you to apply for the American Express Gold Card. And, you know, to be honest I should have done so a while ago.

You've been with us now for [insert number of years] and, in that time, you've been one of our best Personal Cardmembers. Not only have you used the Card regularly, you have also been meticulous about settling your account each month (which is always appreciated). I know that you have also extended the benefits of Cardmembership to your partner.

Now I hope that you, too, are happy with our relationship and the Card you carry at the moment. If you are, then I'd like to tell you a little more about another of our Cards.

You see, I feel that you are at the stage when many people like you naturally incline toward the Gold Card. Perhaps you feel the time is right for you as well.

And so it continued in soft-sell mode for another five paragraphs, until one in ten people who received the letter duly coughed up the £85 for Gold Cardmembership.

This success is easy to explain. Have another look at that copy and you'll see that in the first four paragraphs the words 'you', 'you've' or 'your' appear eighteen times.

As such, it is about the reader's favourite subject. No, not American Express. Them. They are their favourite subject.

The copy also places the reader exactly where they want to be: centre stage.

This reflects well on American Express, for the company demonstrates its understanding of who is the main player in this relationship, and their Cardmember will like them for that.

Finally, speaking of relationships, this is a good lesson in how to talk to existing customers. When next you contact yours, don't do the hard sell. Follow the example above and, having reviewed your relationship, suggest how your customer can get an even better experience or more satisfaction from other products or services in your portfolio.

And another

This is the introduction to the website for the men's clothing brand, Irvine Shirts. Now, all too often you see home pages starting with a banal 'Welcome to . . .' and then trotting out platitudes about the brand's passion and its purpose.

In *Don't Make Me Think*, Steve Krug is scathing about websites that use such 'happy talk . . . the kind of self-congratulatory promotional writing that you find in badly written brochures. Unlike good promotional copy, it conveys no useful information, and it focuses on saying how great we are, as opposed to what makes us great.'[13]

Happily, on the Irvine Shirts site, the man behind the

brand introduces himself but then quickly gets out of the way and shifts attention to the reader – and what he wants.

My name is Alisdair Irvine and I love floral shirts. Maybe I was conceived in Kew Gardens, I dunno, but I've been hooked for years.

If you were to ask me why, I'd respond with this question: Has anyone ever said to you: 'that's a lovely white shirt'? Probably not. But you'll get admiring glances when you wear a floral.

I'd also tell you I've never been a follower of fashion, but I like to dress with distinction. If you feel the same way, then my floral shirts allow you to create your own signature style.

You don't need to be a show-off. Far from it. Just someone who takes pride in your appearance.

You can wear your shirt to enliven a suit or bring panache to a pair of jeans. You can opt for a subtle floral flourish or a design in full fabulous bloom. You're your own stylist.

Like I said, the prospect and not the proprietor is the focus here. As such, Alisdair Irvine behaves like any good shopkeeper would when a potential customer enters his premises.

He gets their attention with the gag about Kew Gardens; interest with the promise of 'admiring glances'; and desire with his references to dressing 'with distinction' and 'your own signature style'.

Next, he addresses the biggest barrier to purchase: the fact that the reader might worry about being thought a show-off in a flamboyant floral. Then he allays such fears by saying, 'You can opt for a subtle floral flourish.'

That last line – 'You're your own stylist' – flatters and empowers the reader. And, incidentally, brings the 'you' and 'your' tally to 15 out of 150 words – or one in every 10.

Hello, ladies . . .

The power of 'you' is also demonstrated in probably the most successful TV script of the century thus far.

It ran in the US and was the launch commercial for the newly repositioned Old Spice. That repositioning had been driven by an insight into just who was buying the products in the Men's Body Wash category.

Contrary to expectation, women were the main purchasers. They were doing so on behalf of their boyfriends and husbands. And what they were buying was stuff that smelt nice to them or, as the script had it: 'lady-scented body wash'.

So Old Spice sent out the great-looking, bare-chested Isaiah Mustafa, a.k.a. 'the man your man could smell like', to talk directly, in his wonderful bass baritone, to the female audience. Here's what he said:

> Hello, ladies. Look at your man, now back to me, now back at your man, now back to me. Sadly, he isn't me. But if he stopped using lady-scented body wash and switched to Old Spice, he could smell like me.
>
> Look down. Back up. Where are you? You're on a boat with the man your man could smell like.
>
> What's in your hand? Back at me. I have it. It's an oyster with two tickets to that thing you love. Look again. The tickets are now diamonds.
>
> Anything is possible when your man smells like Old Spice and not a lady. I'm on a horse.

There you have it. Problem. Solution. Resolution – in just twenty-eight seconds of inspired nonsense. Furthermore, the person at whom it's aimed is addressed directly – 'you' and 'your' feature eight times, or once every three and a half seconds.

Which means there's no mistaking who in the viewing audience is getting their problem solved here.

'You', 'we', 'us' and 'our' make things inclusive

In the Old Spice spot, the product gets just two mentions. And that's enough. As I've said, you should reference the reader or audience three times more than the thing that's being advertised.

When you use 'we', 'us' and 'our' to mean your company, i.e. the provider of the product or service, you risk sounding like a boring blowhard.

But if you use those words to mean you and the reader, then you can create a feeling of shared interest.

English copywriter Tony Brignull made this point when analysing one of the greatest speeches ever made: Abraham Lincoln's Gettysburg Address.

As Brignull explained, 'As president and "chief executive of the nation", it would be understandable if he spoke in the first person singular. The previous speaker had done so at length. But Lincoln doesn't use the word "I" once. Instead he speaks in the plural using "we", "us" and "our" throughout. The effect is inclusive, as if to say we are all in this together.'[14]

In fact, Lincoln used 'our' twice, 'us' three times and 'we' ten times, in a speech that comprised just 271 words.

I've said repeatedly that if you want people to engage with your copy, then you have to get them to see themselves in the story. That's what President Lincoln was doing.

You can apply this to all your dealings with customers, clients and colleagues. In fact, your social life will benefit, too. Suppose you have a hot date this Saturday. If you go to a restaurant, try this. Make sure you talk about your dinner date three times more than you talk about yourself.

Do that, and you'll be waving goodbye on Sunday morning as they rush off to tell their friends they've had a fabulous time with the most fascinating conversationalist they've met in ages.

Use short sentences . . .

Thus far, we've said a lot about the need for simplicity. So I hope the case for short sentences is obvious. It certainly has the weight of academic research behind it.

We can start back in the 1920s, when Harry Kitson published *The Mind of the Buyer*, the first ever psychology-based study of the techniques of marketing.

For Kitson, the length of a sentence determined its complexity. His findings have been supported by numerous other studies, from the Gunning Fog Index of 1952 to the ATOS readability formula of 2000.

However, the daddy of them all is the Flesch-Kincaid Readability Test from the 1970s. And here is Rudolf Flesch explaining what he discovered about short sentences:

'The longer the sentence, the more ideas your mind has to hold in suspense until its final decision on what all the words mean *together*. Longer sentences are more likely to be complex – more subordinate clauses, more prepositional phrases and so on. That means more mental work for the reader. So the longer a sentence, the harder it is to read.'[15]

With easy reading in mind, Flesch recommended that the ideal sentence be between fourteen and sixteen words. Anything between twenty and twenty-five words is just about OK. But if you write above forty words, you'll have lost your reader two lines back.

If you do stray beyond the forty-word mark, then Flesch has this advice for you: 'First, if you want to rewrite a passage . . . you'll have to cut the average sentence length. This means you'll have to break up long, complex sentences and change them to two, three or four shorter ones. In other words, sprinkle periods over your piece of writing.'[16]

If you think that Flesch's findings might be a bit out of date now that we all do most of our reading off a screen, then I should point out that most of what he said has been supported by Jakob Nielsen, the expert in what gets read on the web.

Oops, sorry about that. Chances are, you had difficulty reading that fifty-one-word sentence-cum-paragraph.

Research tells us that when readers get to the end of a long sentence they remember the last bit best. So by the time you got to 'Jakob Nielsen, the expert in what gets read on the web', you'd probably forgotten we started off talking about Rudolf Flesch.

Worse still, you know how we said that the reader starts understanding the sentence when they find the subject and the verb? Well, as this sentence meandered to its close, the chances are you forgot what that subject/verb combo was all about.

So let me re-write that opening paragraph:

Now, you may think that Flesch's findings are a bit out of date. After all, nowadays we do most of our reading off a screen. But most of what he said has been supported by Jakob Nielsen, the expert in what gets read on the web.

That's better, isn't it?

. . . and short paragraphs

Sticking with Jakob Nielsen as our guide, here's what his research revealed about the ideal length for a paragraph: 'Several participants, while scanning text, would read only the first sentence of each paragraph. This suggests that topic sentences are important, as is the "one idea per paragraph" rule. One person who was trying to scan a long paragraph said, "It's not very easy to find that information. They should break that paragraph into two pieces – one for each topic."' [17]

And that's what you should be aiming for. 'One idea per paragraph.' And usually two or three sentences long.

The first sentence introduces the thought, as in: 'Now, you may think that Flesch's findings are a bit out of date.' The second sentence qualifies the original thought: 'After all, nowadays we do most of our reading off a screen,' and the final sentence answers the implied question in the first sentence: 'But most of what he said has been supported by Jakob Nielsen, the expert in what gets read on the web.'

So our point about the continuing validity of Rudolf Flesch's work is made, and we are ready to build on that.

Like I say, three sentences per paragraph should be enough. Or, if you're writing for people reading on their mobile, one is your maximum. For a good example, take a look at Owain Bennallack's posts on The Motley Fool's site.

He never uses industry buzzwords or terminology, even though he is writing about the complex world of investing. Instead he chooses simple, one-syllable words that even a financial numpty like me can understand.

He isn't afraid to use slang, and often refers to 'you'. Indeed, he addresses his reader directly and also anticipates what they might be thinking. For example, 'Now you might argue that wading into a sector in this much distress is madness.'

And, as I said, his paragraphs are always brief – as are his sentences, which means his page looks nice and easy to read.

In short, if he's half as good at playing the markets as he is at writing about them, then you should take his advice.

Step by step until they are where you want them to be

You should certainly copy the way Bennallack limits himself to one thought per paragraph. Then, like him, you'll be able to take your reader with you step by step through your story. Starting with the reader's problem and moving them towards the solution you are offering.

That journey is crucial. But, as we saw on page 86, you also have to begin the story where the reader is attitudinally. And at the beginning they could be sceptical about the claim you are making. Or they might even be downright opposed to your point of view.

By building your argument one paragraph at a time, you are moving them from where they are to where you want them to be. To get them there, you must make sure that every sentence follows logically from one to another.

To an extent, the reader is your ally in this. As a species, we like the linear approach. As Professor Susan Greenfield says, we speak approvingly of people who 'are thinking straight'. To most of us, that is literally the correct mode of thinking.[18]

And, as we've noted, readers are most comfortable with the harmonious balance of cause and effect. They like it when an action described at the beginning of a sentence has a result at its end. Likewise, they are happy when that action prompts another action, a sentence or two along, that takes the story onwards.

By putting the message in sequential order, you make it easier for your reader to predict the way things are going. And the easier it is for the reader to make that prediction, the more likely they are to get to the end of your story.

In short, keeping the momentum going is crucial. But what happens when you need to move an old thought in a different direction, or introduce an entirely new idea? How do you make sure that the reader's stately progress is not halted by a sudden, unavoidable diversion?

Well, one way is to end a paragraph with a question about what has just gone before. If that question is one which the reader might well be asking themselves at that moment, then their curiosity will carry them on to the next paragraph.

But are there other tactics you can employ?

Use these linking words and phrases

Linking words and phrases are the glue that hold your sentences together. By and large they have two purposes.

Firstly, they tell the reader that the next sentence is going to build on the thought contained in the last sentence they read.

So, for example, you can use 'firstly'. It is a linking word because you can only use it after a sentence which tells the reader that a list of supporting facts or information is on its way. By the same token, you can use 'secondly', 'thirdly', 'fourth' and 'fifth', all the way up to 'finally'.

'So' and 'for example' and 'for instance' are also linking words that tell your reader that the next sentence is going to expand on what came before. You can also use 'and', 'for', 'moreover', 'what's more', 'because', 'likewise', 'therefore', 'better still', 'on the subject of', 'speaking of which', 'in addition', 'similarly', 'apparently', 'consequently', 'suffice to say', 'as a result' and 'by the same token'.

Indeed, you can use 'indeed', 'in short', 'of course' and 'in fact'.

Conversely, you can use linking words to let the reader know that the next sentence is going to challenge, question or contradict what has gone before.

For example, 'conversely', 'on the other hand', 'unfortunately', 'having said that', 'despite that/this' and 'however'.

And finally, if you want to move the argument on to another subject but still keep the flow going, you can use these linking words: 'but', 'either way', 'anyway', 'meanwhile', 'at the same time', 'in conclusion', 'be that as it may' and 'whichever'.

Whichever linking word or phrase you use, be sure to

pop it into your sentence before the reader gets to the verb. If you insert it *after* the verb then the reader will already have used the verb to predict where the sentence is heading, and your signpost will come too late to guide them.

Now I know that one or two of you wince when starting sentences with 'and', 'for', 'so' and other conjunctions. So bear this in mind: the best-read book in all of English literature, the King James Bible, is so readable precisely because it is full of linking words. Consider St Matthew Chapter 6, verses 28–33:

> And why take ye thought for raiment? Consider the lilies of the field, how they grow; they toil not, neither do they spin:
>
> And yet I say unto you, That even Solomon in all his glory was not arrayed as one of these.
>
> Wherefore if God so clothe the grass of the field, which today is, and tomorrow is cast into the oven, shall he not much more clothe you, O ye of little faith?
>
> Therefore take no thought saying 'What shall we eat?' or 'What shall we drink?' or 'Wherewithall shall we be clothed?'
>
> (For after all these things do the Gentiles seek:) for your heavenly Father knoweth that you have need of all these things.
>
> But seek you first the kingdom of God, and his righteousness; and all these things will be added to you.
>
> Amen.

8:

YOUR THIRD DRAFT:
CUT THESE THINGS OUT

That's your second draft out of the way, and it's time for a breather.

Yes, I know you'll be up against the clock, but try to build this break into your schedule. You'll benefit and, more importantly, so will your writing.

The longer you leave it the better. Because, when you come back to your copy and look at it in cold blood, you'll see it through the eyes of your reader. You won't remember what you wrote, so, like your reader, you won't know what's coming next. Therefore you'll have to work out where the story is going based on the last thing you read.

However, the copy can't be so predictable it becomes boring. It has to keep telling you useful and interesting things you didn't already know. So keep checking all this is happening.

Along the way, you'll also bump into words and phrases that made it in there when you were bashing out your first draft. This is my fault. I said you needed to write quickly and not be too self-critical.

However, that was then and this is now. And now's the time for the red pencil.

Let's start with jargon

We ended the last chapter with a quote from the King James Bible. This wonderful book is full of words and phrases that are nowadays used only by vicars, ministers and priests addressing their flock.

Which begs the question, if you're writing to a vicar or priest, do you throw in some of their jargon in order to establish a rapport? Likewise, if you're writing to an IT specialist, finance director, wine buff or a woman who likes bingo?

I don't think so. As I've said, you should try to write as you speak, and that's hard to do if you are using words and phrases you're not sure of. If you misuse the jargon, your reader will infer that you don't understand them – and your chance of winning them over will be gone.

So be careful.

There are some callings and professions, like the Church and the law, that can be excused a certain amount of jargon. Their terminology has ancient roots. And there are others, like those who work in IT and engineering, whose everyday language is technical.

But most other people who write and talk in a fashion peculiar to their group are suspect. Because their use of jargon usually has one of two dubious purposes.

People will think you're hiding something

Let me give you an example of dubious purpose #1. I had a colleague who often started spouting jargon when he felt challenged by a client. Going forward, I knew we were far from a win-win situation when he began drilling down, getting granular, shifting his paradigm and calling for greater transparency across all touchpoints.

He'd have been better off saying 'we've messed up, I'm sorry'.

A similar act of truthful contrition might have saved Citigroup's blushes a few years back. After a particularly bad string of quarterly results, the bank's board opted for a cost-saving campaign that entailed firing thousands of staff.

Not that they were willing to admit this brutal fact. Here's their press release's headline: 'Citigroup Announces Repositioning Action to Further Reduce Expenses and Improve Efficiency'.

And this is its first paragraph: 'Citigroup today announced a series of repositioning actions that will further reduce expenses and improve efficiency across the company while maintaining Citi's unique capabilities to serve clients especially in the emerging markets. This action will result in increased buying efficiency, streamlining operations and an optimized consumer footprint across geographies.'

And here's what the journalist at *Forbes* magazine wrote: 'The Citigroup Bloodbath: New CEO Cuts 11,000 Jobs.'[1]

That journalist sensed something even smellier beneath the press release's steaming verbiage. If you use jargon, your readers will detect the whiff of bullshit, too.

You'll come across as insecure

Dishonest people use jargon. So, too, do the insecure. They fear that if they are easily understood people won't take them seriously. So they camouflage their meaning in the hope that it will lend authority to their ideas and mystique to their role.

Daniel Kahneman sets them straight in *Thinking, Fast and Slow*: 'If you care about being thought credible and intelligent, do not use complex language where simpler language will do. My Princeton colleague Danny Oppenheimer refuted a myth prevalent among undergraduates about the vocabulary that professors find most impressive. In an article titled "Consequences of Erudite Vernacular Utilized Irrespective of Necessity: Problems with Using Long Words Needlessly", he showed that couching familiar ideas in pretentious language is taken as a sign of poor intelligence and low credibility.'[2]

Let that be a lesson to us marketing folk who might be tempted to reconfigure the brand ecosystem. Or recommend cross-platform personalization in full-funnel marketing suites. And as for ideating about today's social plasma and its five crucial elements: customer-managed relationships, curated social engagement, mobile convergence, gamification and . . .

The above jargon is pretty hardcore, and comes from agencies pitching clients who speak the same gibberish. But, to a greater or lesser degree, we're all guilty. 'Relevant abruption', anyone?

I'd rise to its defence but concede that if we don't want to come across as insecure airheads, we should avoid 'disruptive experiential and immersive strategies' and resist the temptation to 'fast-track', 'ring-fence', 'roll out' or 'benchmark' our 'keydrivers', 'stakeholders', 'customer bases' and 'user groups'.

Terminology like this damages credibility. Unfortunately, a reliance on jargon sometimes has more dire consequences.

After the 7/7 London bombings of 2005, the coroner found there were delays in caring for the victims because different emergency services had been unable to understand each other's jargon.

In response, the various emergency services got together to make sure this never happened again. After much discussion they decided that what was needed was an 'Emergency Responder Interoperability Lexicon' which could be 'cascaded' through various training courses.

Oh dear.

Avoid clichés like the plague

And old jokes like the one above.

But are clichés really that bad? I mean, I said back in chapter 6 that we should write as we speak. And it is entirely possible that in conversation I might say I am going to avoid something 'like the plague'. So why is it so wrong for me to write it?

Well, I also said that we should write as we speak *when we are concentrating hard on the conversation we are having*. And if we are concentrating that hard, we'll avoid previously prepared phrases that stop us from saying exactly what we mean.

For that's what clichés are: the literary equivalent of instant pot noodle – a lazy alternative to creating something original and satisfying.

If, however, you are tempted by this junk food of the English language, add your own seasoning and cook up something new.

Here's an example from an online recruitment ad for the

travel company Brown + Hudson. The copy is explaining how creative and innovative the new recruit will have to be: 'We have to think laterally, sideways, upside down and so far out of the box that it's long ago been tidied away and put in a cupboard by the cleaners.'

I saw a similar act of reinvention a couple of weeks ago. A friend asked me to proofread and sense-check a book he's written about advertising. It was an enlightening read, and there was little need for the red pencil.

However, on the first page he'd said that 'because of complicated agency processes, getting work out nowadays was like wading through treacle'. I mentioned to him that no one has actually bought a tin of treacle for thirty years. Which indicated that this expression might be a little tired.

He immediately proposed 'swimming through hummus', which was a more vivid way of bringing his thought to life.

And the same goes for abstractions

Next time you find yourself reaching for a cliché, think about what it is you really want to say and then say it. Likewise, if you find you've written 'retail outlet', 'leisure amenity' or 'employment opportunity', delete such abstractions and replace them with 'shop', 'pub' and 'job'.

And take inspiration from something I saw last February when driving through North Queensland. There by the roadside was a sign offering a 'Big Shed to Rent'. How refreshing.

I suppose we should expect such a tell-it-like-it-is approach from a country where the two most important geological regions are named 'The Great Sandy Desert' and 'The Snowy Mountains'. But, I know that back in the UK, the 'Big Shed' would've been an 'Extensive Storage Facility'. Descriptions like that are not just vague. Psycholinguists tell us that, unlike concrete words like 'Big Shed', abstract terms are much harder to store in the biggest shed of them all, your reader's long-term memory.

Similarly, if you're tempted to write 'the [insert noun] situation, procedures, framework or learnings' and describe the subsequent 'outcomes', the reader loses track of your argument and quickly forgets what little of it they ever grasped.

There is something fundamentally inhuman about such terminology. It makes copy look like it was written by software programmed with abstractions that have only entered the language in the past twenty years.

And no one likes it. To use that irritating buzzword, people want 'authenticity'.

I think that's what we've been striving for. But we've described it as seeing the world through our reader's eyes, and writing as we speak.

Correct your inaccuracies

This kind of conversational style is fine. But when we speak, in our haste, we sometimes opt for the wrong word. So as you read your copy, keep asking, 'Is this really what I meant to say?'

Here's an example from my first draft. On page 108 I wrote: 'The right words are those that make your meaning clear. And the way to achieve this kind of clarity is by using the most popular words in the English language.'

Hmmm. By writing 'the most popular', I seemed to be

advising you to use words that appear on some list of the 'Fifty Best-Loved Words in the English Language'. And that's not what I meant.

So I replaced that with, 'The right words are those that make your meaning clear. And the way to achieve this kind of clarity is by using words in common parlance.' But then I realized that, stupidly enough, with 'in common parlance' I'd chosen a term that people rarely use, and might not understand.

So I went with: 'The right words are those that make your meaning clear. And the best are the ones we use all the time.' Which I think most of you will get.

Alas, this is just one of dozens of amendments I've had to make.

For example, on page 7, I was trying to explain 'confirmation bias' and said that it was 'your reader's inability to believe anything that contradicts their preconceptions'. But when I re-read this, it seemed wrong for three reasons: saying it was an 'inability' meant that it was something that couldn't be overcome, and that's not true. Saying it was an inability to 'believe anything' is a misleading exaggeration. And using the word 'preconceptions' was dangerous because I'm not entirely sure what it means.

So I changed it to 'your reader's unwillingness to accept things that run counter to their point of view'. Which is not only more accurate, but simpler.

A small change can make a big difference

Sometimes you'll come across things you've written that make sense to you, but need another word or two or a bit of restructuring in order to make your point clearer.

Here's an example from page 12. I was explaining what made an effective headline and I wrote: 'If the headline arouses curiosity, that's good. And if you need to know why curiosity works in a headline, just take a look at BuzzFeed's popularity.'

In retrospect that gave only an impressionistic explanation. I knew what I meant (I think), but I was worried the reader wouldn't get my meaning. So, I changed it to: 'If the headline arouses curiosity, that's good because we are a curious species. If you're in doubt, just look at the popularity of BuzzFeed. Only an innate curiosity would explain why three million of us want to see "22 Celebrity Cat Ladies and Dog Dads Who Will Melt Your Cold Dead Heart".'

Sometimes, slapdash writing gets between you and your reader. In my early drafts I had this: 'Well, according to Caples that brings us to the most effective headline of them all . . .'

But that reads as if Caples thinks we have arrived at the most effective headline of all. Which is unlikely, because John Caples has been dead for over twenty-five years and no longer has much interest in where we are in our search for the right headline.

What I meant to say was, 'Well, that brings us to the kind of headline that, according to John Caples, is the most effective of them all.'

Make sure your subheads are as clear as can be

Sometimes you find that, in your haste, you've written the daftest things.

On page 95, you'll see the subhead 'Give them the facts'. Would you believe that this started life as 'Just the facts, Ma'am'?

Eh?

Well, 'Just the facts, Ma'am' is a quote from the 1950s American cop show *Dragnet*, and when I came to write the subhead for that section it just popped into my head, and a split-second later was up there on the screen.

I'm glad it's not there any more. Because subheads are there to give a clear indication of the story being told beneath. And it's unwise to use them to display your knowledge of obscure television catchphrases that only one in 5,000 of your readers might appreciate.

Finally, amongst my many howlers was this.

In my first draft I was writing about the reader's need to know where the story is going. I tried to summarize this by saying, 'And their ability to anticipate that direction is absolutely crucial if they are to persist with the narrative.'

Which kind of said what I meant, but the big words I'd used towered over the sentence and blocked out the light of meaning. So I changed them to:

'And the easier it is for them to tell where the story is heading, the more likely they are to read on.' Which, I hope you agree, is better.

Incidentally, at that point I realized how pretentious I sounded using 'narrative' instead of 'story'. So I set about switching those words whenever I came across them.

Anyway, there were dozens more examples of unclear and inaccurate writing in drafts number one . . . two . . . three . . . four . . . (and there are almost certainly quite a few in this one). To divert further criticism from me, here's an example from the DMA's survey of 433 copywriters that I referred to on page 29.

If you don't correct your mistakes, no one else will

I said back then that the UK's copywriters were down in the dumps because no one respects their skills.

One of them explained why. And, in recommending a corrective, did a very good job of illustrating the cause: 'Copywriters need to be put on a pedestal the same as great designers and developers do. Unfortunately, because most people can write in one form or another it's not seen as difficult a skill to find. But because bosses, clients etc often have no idea how to put code together they see it as magic in comparison. Clients, agencies, bosses whoever need education as to what copywriting really is and it's worth.'[3]

My advice here is, 'Physician, heal thyself'. Because a quick re-read would have rooted out the half-dozen childish mistakes that reside in those six lines of copy.

Here's another example of how a writer would have benefited from asking, 'Is this really what I mean to say?' It comes from a poster I noticed in Chicago's O'Hare International Airport. It featured a picture of a child's teddy bear covering its eyes, alongside the headline: 'No one should have to witness the sexual abuse of children'.

Now, I may be getting the wrong end of the stick here,

but this headline seems to accept that child abuse will happen, but draws the line at anyone having to watch it. Indeed, according to this ad, the victim isn't the child, the victim is the viewer; and I'm pretty sure that wasn't what the writer meant.

That this kind of thing gets into print is a warning to us all. If you don't spot your mistakes, no one will come to your rescue.

Nor is it enough to think, 'I know what I mean, and assume that the reader will figure it out.' They won't make the effort to wrestle your intended meaning from the tangle of nouns and verbs you've given them. They'll simply stop reading – or worse still, they might take the wrong message away and, in the above case, go in search of a child to abuse (in private, of course).

Cut the superfluous

In the examples above, I've shown how a few well-chosen extra words can make your meaning clearer to the reader.

But your job doesn't end there. When you are re-reading your copy, you should also look for ways to bring not just clarity but concision to what you have written.

Over the years I've found that in most cases you can take the red pencil to up to 25 per cent of the text and not lose one iota of meaning. Indeed, cutting away in this fashion will enable you to make the flow of your copy a lot smoother.

As the man said, 'Less is more.'

When you first start the exercise, you'll wonder where the cuts can possibly come from. But once you get going, you'll recognize the words, sentences and whole paragraphs that are adding little to the message you are trying to convey.

It is simply a matter of having the time to edit your original draft. As the seventeenth-century polymath Blaise Pascal is reputed to have written in a postscript to a friend: 'I'm sorry I wrote you such a long letter, I didn't have time to write you a short one.'

In order to do it properly, you will also need to look at your copy through a fresh pair of eyes. So, once again, I'd strongly advise you to lay your writing aside for a few hours or a day or two before re-reading it again.

Let's have another go at that, shall we?

That's the theory. Now let's see how much I can cut from the copy that came after 'Cut the superfluous'. Here we go:

In the examples above, I've shown how extra words and sentences can make your meaning clearer.

But your job doesn't end there. When you re-read your copy, you should be looking for ways to make it shorter.

Often, you can cut as much as 25 per cent and not lose one iota of meaning. Indeed, cutting makes your copy flow smoother.

When you start, you'll wonder where the cuts can come. But you'll soon recognize the words, sentences and paragraphs that add little to your message.

You need time to edit your original draft (as French polymath Blaise Pascal said: 'I'm sorry I wrote you such a long letter, I didn't have time to write you a short one.')

And you also need to look at your copy through fresh

eyes. So, again, I advise you to lay your writing aside for as long as possible before re-reading it.

OK, that's the re-write over

The original was 244 words long and the new version is 149. So I've cut it by nearly 40 per cent and, as I hope you agree, not lost any of the meaning.

You'll find some easy kills in the original. Instead of 'in order to', just write 'to'. Instead of 'in most cases', write 'often'. And drop the 'first' from 'first start'.

'Over the years', 'you're conveying' and 'once again' are all redundant. As to 'less is more', it's been used so many times it's lost all its flavour. It's like putting extra oats into your muesli.

I was tempted to get rid of Pascal, too. His quote is used a lot in this context, but it did make a serious point. So he stayed in. Just.

And finally, the original last paragraph was mostly waffle, and much deserving of the axe.

When you're writing, there are lots of common phrases you should be sharpening your blade for. 'New innovations' and 'new developments' are my favourites. Has anyone ever come up with an old innovation or an old development? *Whack*.

How about 'consensus of opinion'? Just write 'opinion'. 'Hold a meeting?' Go with 'meeting'. 'Take action?' Try 'act'. 'In reference to' – opt for 'regarding'. And as to 'in-depth analysis', be content with 'analysis'.

Finally, there's another simple way to drastically reduce

your word count. Take out adjectives such as 'simple' and adverbs such as 'drastically'. They didn't add much to the meaning of the previous sentence, did they?

Don't, however, purge all adjectives and adverbs. They are, despite what Stephen King told us on page 117, valuable tools if used sparingly. As I did with 'valuable' and 'sparingly' just then.

Read your work out loud

After all these revisions, there's one last thing you need to do. Check your tone of voice is natural and conversational.

There's a simple way of doing this. Read it out loud. If you find there are words and phrases that you wouldn't say face to face, rewrite them.

There are other benefits. As David Abbott pointed out, 'Like many copywriters, I read my copy out loud as I write. It helps me check the rhythm of the line and ultimately the flow of the whole piece. I often adopt the appropriate accent or tone, though my general "reading voice" is laughably mid-Atlantic.'[4]

Incidentally, this technique was used by a master craftsman in another field of mass communications. Frank Sinatra, the finest interpreter of the popular song, also read his lyrics out loud. This enabled him to get the inflections right and achieve the conversational delivery that characterized his style. To hear what I mean, pour a Jack Daniels and google his 'Medley: The Gal that Got Away – It Never Entered My Mind'. But not yet – we've got a book to finish.

Let's get back to David Abbott and his adoption of an American accent. For a writer who could talk one on one with Middle England better than any other, this seems strange.

But maybe here's why he did it: in his formative years, the mid 1960s, he did a stint at Doyle Dane Bernbach, New York. It was there that he picked up the informal, personal style that was pioneered at that agency. So powerful was the hold that DDB had on the creative imagination in the 1960s that, years later, Abbott was perhaps still hearing his mentors' voices as he read his copy back to himself.

If that's the case, then it brings us to the next thing you need to do.

Get the opinion of someone you respect

Once you've checked your copy through and made all the changes I've suggested above, get a second opinion. But choose someone who has an opinion worth getting.

They need to be smart enough to see the flaws in your work, and confident enough to point them out to you.

As Proverbs 28.23 tells us, 'Honest correction is appreciated more than flattery.'

When I was writing my biography of US adman Howard Gossage, I wanted a second opinion from someone who knew about the industry in the 1960s. So I asked the veteran copywriter Andrew Cracknell to read the manuscript. His book about advertising in that decade, *The Real Mad Men*, had just been published, so he seemed the most knowledgeable person I could ask.

He could only bring himself to read half of it. As he said, it was a hagiography and not worth finishing.

This may not have been the critique I wanted, but it was

certainly the critique I needed. And I re-read the manuscript with fresh eyes, then set about turning the plaster saint into a human being.

You'd be wise to find your own Andrew Cracknell. And when you do, make sure they understand what they are looking at.

Show them the brief you were working from. Failing that, explain who the target audience is. What it is you're selling. What problem it will solve. And what is the proposition you are making to your reader.

Finally, give them the other thing they'll need. Time. Don't rush up and say, 'This thing has to go in twenty minutes, whaddya think?' Allow them to read it at their leisure.

Once they've done that, take time to listen to what they have to say. Write notes, ask questions, find out if there were any bits they didn't fully understand. Accept that they might be being polite, so tease out the real reasons they don't like it.

Then thank them. And begin the next stage of the process.

9:
REWRITE

There's not much I can help you with here. I don't know what you were told to change. So crack on, but make sure you give yourself enough time to do it properly.

The best writers are usually obsessive tweakers. Alice Lowe, who ran Howard Gossage's agency, told me that he would still be re-writing ads on the morning they appeared in the *New York Times*.

So stick at it and, once you've finished, I'll see you on the next page.

The next page?

Well, yes, your job's not over yet.

It isn't enough to write clearly. If you want your reader to notice your work, engage with it and do what you want them to do, then there's something else you need to know.

10:

HOW TO LAY YOUR COPY OUT

Way back on page 83, I said you should write as you speak when you are concentrating hard on the conversation you are having.

But suppose you *are* in a conversation and you have a thick Glaswegian accent, while the person you are talking to is an American. Chances are the poor lass will understand only one word in every four.

Which means, while your argument might be irrefutable, your delivery will be incomprehensible.

When it comes to presenting that message in written form, you are faced with the same barriers. However, while the Glaswegian cannot help having an impenetrable accent, you have no excuse for laying out your copy badly. So to make it as legible and understandable as possible, follow the dos and don'ts below.

What's the difference between layouts for web and for print?

To answer this, I've compared the views of the two Lords of Layout: Jakob Nielsen, who has spent over twenty years studying how to get read on the web, and Colin Wheildon, who wrote the bible on how to do a print layout, *Type and Layout: Are You Communicating – Or Just Making Pretty Shapes*?

Both used eye-tracking studies and reached much the same conclusion on how to create a page that is easy to scan. They insisted on:

- headlines that stand out
- subheads
- short paragraphs
- white space between the paragraphs.

They also recommended other magnetic elements (as Nielsen calls them), such as captions under photographs, postscripts in letters and, as we'll see below, putting important words in bold and making bullet-pointed lists.

These tactics encourage the scanner to stay longer and become a reader. But what happens then?

Well, here's Nielsen and Wheildon's advice on how to make your copy legible and comprehensible. Other experts chip in, too.

While we'll come across one or two bones of contention, let's kick off with a tip that everybody seems to agree on.

Don't put white words on a dark page or screen

Light type on a dark background might be OK for short headlines. But when it comes to the kind of body copy you're reading now, avoid it.

If you use white lettering on a dark setting, the light bounces off the white shapes and blurs the definition of the words on the page or screen.

Conversely, black letters absorb the light and cause the reader less eye strain.

So never reverse white type out of black – unless, of course, you are hiding bad news that you do not want people to read.

Don't use a small type size

There's also a consensus on the importance of the size of the type you use. Choose a point size that the person you are writing for can read comfortably. And, as Jakob Nielsen advises, if you're writing for the web, 'allow users to change the font size'.[1]

Unfortunately, I cannot dictate the font size the publisher of this book will use. However, I have written the manuscript in 11-point Arial. It is easy to read both on the screen and when I print it off.

Does that mean that 11-point size is a good rule of thumb? No. Typefaces come in different sizes. For example, 11-point Arial is considerably bigger than 11-point Times New Roman.

It's all down to the size of the 'x' in the typeface's alphabet. If the 'x' is large, that means every letter will be big relative to those in a typeface whose 'x' is smaller.

Use a typeface that's been created for the screen

So choosing a typeface with a bigger 'x' can make it easier for people to read your copy. But why stop there? If your work is going to appear on a laptop, tablet or mobile, choose a typeface that was created specifically for the screen.

In the 1990s Matthew Carter created Verdana, Tahoma, Nina and George for just this purpose. More recently, David Barlow at the Font Bureau has been making new fonts for the web and adapting old ones so they are easier on the eye when on screen. For example, his PoynterSerif RE has a larger 'x' size and each letter is wider than its counterpart in the version used for print.

Choose an easy-to-read typeface

Both versions of PoynterSerif RE are plain typefaces that are easy to read. And unless, for example, you are editing a newsletter aimed at 𝕲𝖔𝖙𝖍𝖘, these plain faces are the kind you should choose.

This is especially so if you are asking the reader to do something. Suppose you are trying to persuade a client to adopt a new way of briefing you. If you use an easy-to-read typeface to explain the new process, they will think it's easy to perform.

However, if you choose an overly elaborate typeface, like *Corsiva*, for example, then it will be hard to read. And as a result, the reader will feel the task is difficult, too.

Speaking of easy- and hard-to-read fonts . . .

Should you use a serif face . . .

You will probably know this, but just in case you don't, the serifs are the little feet at the bottom of the f, h, i, k, l, m, n, p, q, r. And the extensions at the top of the 'v' and 'w'.

For capitals, you can see these decorative extensions on the A, B, C, D, E, F, G, H, I, J, K, L, M, N, O, P, Q, R, S, T, U, V, W, X, Y and Z.

On the other hand, a sans serif face is one that is without these ornamental feet and extensions.

In *Type and Layout*, Colin Wheildon came out whole-heartedly for the serif face. After one test, he reported that five times more readers achieved good comprehension with serif type than with sans serif.[2]

Given that every daily newspaper in the UK uses a serif face for headlines and text, it would appear that, on this point, all their publishers agree with Wheildon.

. . . or a sans serif face?

Then again, most magazines are set in sans serif, as are the majority of websites. The latter can be partially explained by the fact that Jakob Nielsen has argued for sans serif. Other experts feel the same way. In *Reading Letters: Designing for Legibility*, Sophie Beier says, 'It is time to abandon any rigid belief that serifs are always better and adopt a more nuanced view on the use of both serif and sans serif type-faces.'[3]

The fact that such sans serif faces as Tahoma and Verdana have been created to improve legibility on the web shows how opinion has shifted.

Be that as it may, research by Gerard Unger indicates that a serif face is still more helpful. To understand why, we need to revisit what the eye does when we are reading. On page 4 we saw that we read by fixing on the text for a split second and taking in about seven to nine letters. We then jump forward a few more letters before another brief period of fixation.

However, that's not all our eyes are doing.

Our understanding of what we're reading lies in our ability to predict what's coming next. And that is enhanced by our peripheral vision. While we focus on the seven to nine letters in front of us, out of the corner of our eye we are checking out the next fifteen letters. And, according to Gerard Unger, the serifs on the extremes of ascending and descending characters make it easier for us to recognize those letters.[4]

In short, what would otherwise be hazy is clear. And given that we've been striving for clarity throughout this book, perhaps we should use a serif face whenever we can.

Should you use CAPITAL LETTERS?

As with the serif and sans serif debate, the conventional wisdom on this question has been challenged recently. Whereas once we were told that capitals (or upper-case) are less legible, some experts now say there's no difference.

However, while they may be just as legible, we still read capitals slowly. According to Sofie Beier, 'Many reading speed studies have found upper-case letters to perform badly, as few readers are used to reading long passages of text set in upper-case letters.'[5]

So that's one good reason to avoid it. Here's another: upper case on the web comes across as shouting. And readers think it's rude.

Not that that stopped Microsoft from introducing an all-capital-letter menu for its Visual Studio 2012. Irate complaints flooded in, in lower case. The ironic ones came in upper.

How about using
- *italics*
- **bold**
- and bullet points?

Like sans serif, *italics* were long considered hard to read. Colin Wheildon came to their rescue when he found that, 'while readers initially paused when confronted with an unusual face, italics caused them no difficulty at all'.[6]

Bold, on the other hand, was more tricky. He discovered that long text in bold tested badly.

However, he found that it was good for highlighting words and phrases that might attract the casual browser at scanning stage.[7]

You will notice that I have only used bold for subheads in this book. That's because I don't like this tactic. As I've said, you should write as you speak, and emboldening certain words indicates you are shouting those words. Which is something I rarely do in conversation, and would never do to people I am trying to sell to.

I have a similar thing about bullet-pointed lists. But Jakob Nielsen loves them for web pages, and reckons that readers feel that way, too: 'Bulleted lists, when well done, are extremely attractive elements. The eye goes to them frequently. In fact, people looked at 70% of the bulleted lists they encountered.'[8]

So, that puts me in my place. I think, however, that I'm right about what's coming up next.

Avoid using too MANY different typefaces, weights and sizes

When people are scanning your copy, they are confused by these inconsistencies. That's because each style is fighting for the reader's attention.

Moreover, if the copy is your spoken voice in print then a level of consistency is necessary in order for the reader to 'hear' you properly. If you have too many shifts in emphasis and tone then, quite frankly, you come across as bonkers.

I'm assuming you're not bonkers, so the general rule is three font choices or less per project.

Should you make the length of the line of type as wide as this is?

Or is it better for the line to be narrower?

The gurus favour the latter. Jakob Nielsen prefers multiple narrow columns to one long line of type.[9]

Colin Wheildon said that 'Thirty-eight per cent of readers found body type set wider than about 60 characters hard to read. A further twenty-two per cent indicated that they probably wouldn't read wide measure body type even though they didn't find any difficulty reading it.'[10]

On the other hand, Professor Mary C. Dyson's research into onscreen reading supports longer line lengths. She found that lines of around one hundred characters were read fastest. Apparently that burst of speed is explained by our eyes flowing uninterrupted along the length of the line.

Shorter lines cause us to stop more often as we return to the left-hand margin.

Not that this jumping back and forth seems to bother us. As Professor Dyson concedes, 'people prefer a more moderate line length'.[11] And adds that our comprehension levels are higher when we are reading narrower columns.[12]

Which, again, is something that the UK's newspaper publishers seem to have known for some time. And if it's good enough for those who live and die by readership figures, then I'd suggest you follow suit and give your readers what they want.

Ragged right and left

According to Colin Wheildon, having your headlines or subheads centred like this and therefore having them appear what is called 'ragged' on the right-hand side and 'ragged' on the left-hand side is OK.
But he says you should not do it for the blocks of text that come beneath the headlines or subheads.
That's because your reader has to make a different jump back to the left-hand margin every time they want to start a new line. And after a short while this becomes tiresome and, as we know, anything that makes it difficult for the reader should be avoided.[13]

Your reader will find it much easier if there is a fixed starting point on the left-hand side of your copy. Or 'justified' as it's known.

When you are writing body copy, the only time you should stray from the fixed left-hand margin is at the start of your paragraphs.

As you see, I have indented mine. Why? Because this

gives the reader a jump start into the paragraph, thus keeping them moving through the copy. It also shortens the distance the eye has to travel from the final word in one paragraph to the first word in the next. And, as we know, anything that makes it easier for the reader is a good thing.

And that's it: how to lay your copy out in a way that encourages a person to notice it, scan it and keep reading. I've mentioned clear headlines, subheads, using bold type . . . that kind of thing. But, right at the end, there's another element that'll catch a person's eye: a P.S.

P. S. THAT WAS THE THEORY.
BUT WHAT ABOUT THE PRACTICE?

To write better copy, that's precisely what you need to do. Practise. The more you write, the better you'll get. It's how good writers become good.

In his brilliant book *The Elements of Eloquence*, Mark Forsyth makes this encouraging observation: 'Shakespeare got better and better and better, which was easy because he started badly.'[1]

You might reply, 'That's fine. Will was an actor and had plenty of time on his hands while resting between parts. Where do I get the time to practise my writing?'

Well, I'd suggest you have plenty of opportunities. You're just not taking them.

Practise on the boss's time . . .

In 2015, some 205 billion emails were sent and received.[2]

That's not 205 billion throughout the year. Nor is it per month. That's 205 billion emails a day.

Apparently, your share of this was 122. And, of them, you wrote and sent an average of thirty-four. That's thirty-four chances a day to practise your craft.[3]

Most of us pass up these opportunities. We dash off our

message, often without a salutation or a sign-off. And send it without re-reading it, or running the spell check.

But if we just sat back for a few minutes and thought about who we were writing to and what we wanted them to do or feel, then our emails would be much better.

And if we factored in the problem/solution dynamic and the proposition we were making, then how much more engaging and effective they'd be.

I know you're busy, but try picking one email a day and giving it the thought it deserves. Then choose another the next day. Leaving time between sessions in this way is called 'spaced practice', and educational psychologists say it's the best way to learn.[4]

. . . and on me

If you're already putting a lot of effort into your emails, then I apologize for suggesting otherwise. But I still believe you'll improve if you do the things I've explained in this book.

We can all get better at writing. And that undoubtedly applies to yours truly. Indeed, if you have any observations or criticisms of this book, then I'd like to read them.

So, start practising your craft right now and email me: harrisosteve@googlemail.com

And if you fancy the beer I mentioned on page 47, I'm up for that, too.

Notes

1: What You Really Want is 'Effective' Copy

1 Bob Hoffman, *Marketers Are from Mars, Consumers Are from New Jersey* (San Francisco: Type A Group, 2015), p. 65.
2 YouGov, 'Ad-blocking Software Poses Challenge to Advertisers, Brands and Publishers', 18 November 2015, https://yougov.co.uk/news/2015/11/18/consumers-and-advertising-making-it-all-add/.
3 Jakob Nielsen, 'Legibility, Readability, and Comprehension: Making Users Read Your Words', 15 November 2015, https://www.nngroup.com/articles/legibility-readability-comprehension/.
4 Stephen King, *On Writing: A Memoir of the Craft* (London: Hodder, 2012; first published New York, 2000), p. 184.
5 Sarah Vizard, 'Marketers Living in La-La Land by Mistaking Awareness for Conversion', *Marketing Week*, 24 September 2015.
6 Ibid.
7 *New Scientist*, 'Why Things Fall Apart', 15 August 2015.

2: The Thinking Before the Writing

1 B. Schwartz, A. Ward, J. Monterosso, S. Lyumbomirsky, K. White, D. R. Lehman, 'Maximizing versus Satisfying: Happiness Is a Matter of Choice', *Journal of Personality and Social Psychology*, 2002 (83) pp. 1178–97.
2 *The Copy Book: How Some of the Best Advertising Writers in the World Write Their Advertising* (London: Taschen, 2011), p. 200.
3 Ibid., p. 216.
4 *Advertising Age*, 'Gossage Tells Clinic Advertising is America's Only Original Art Form', 16 February 1959.

5 Martin Weigel, 'The Fracking of Attention', *Canalside View*, 27 October 2015, http://martinweigel.org/2015/10/27/the-fracking-of-attention/.

6 Niki Chesworth, 'How to Survive the Email Overload', *Evening Standard*, 5 November 2015.

7 John Caples, *Tested Advertising Methods* (Upper Saddle River, NJ: Prentice Hall, 1997), p. 17.

8 *Today's Trucking*, 'Epic Numbers of Volvo Truck Sales', 18 December 2013, http://www.todaystrucking.com/epic-numbers-of-volvo-truck-sales.

9 Charlie Porter, 'Nike's New Moves', *Financial Times*, 26 March/ 27 March 2016.

10 John Yorke, *Into the Woods: How Stories Work and Why We Tell Them* (London: Penguin, 2013), pp. 3–4.

11 Ibid., pp. 8–9.

12 Helen Edwards, 'Don't Drown Your Consumers in an Ocean of Branded Pap', *Marketing*, 5 November 2014.

3: How to Write Your Brief

1 Bob Hoffman, *Marketers Are from Mars, Consumers Are from New Jersey* (San Francisco: Type A Group, 2015), p. 17.

2 Thomas Tamblyn, 'Airbnb's Passive Aggressive Ad Campaign in San Francisco Has Spectacularly Backfired', *Huffington Post*, 22 October 2015.

3 Richard Branson, *The Virgin Way: Everything I Know About Leadership* (London: Virgin Books, 2014), p. 82.

4 Andy Reinhardt, 'Steve Jobs: "There's Sanity Returning"', *Business Week*, 25 May 1998.

5 Lucy Tesseras, 'Knowledge is Power for Customers' Top 100 Brands', *Marketing Week*, 10 September 2015, p. 15.

4: Getting Your Message in the Right Order

1 Andy Maslen, *Online Copywriting that Sells: How to Write Web Copy So Powerful People Can't Help Buying From You* (Sunfish, 2006), p. 19.

2 Neil Patel, *How to Make Visitors Read Your Entire Article*,

18 January 2016, http://contentmarketinginstitute.com/2016/01/visitors-read-article/.

3 Interview with Jerry Mander, 14 March 2011.

5: How to Write Your Headline

1 David Ogilvy, *Confessions of an Advertising Man* (New York: Atheneum, 1984; first published New York, 1963), p. 104.

2 Kara Pernice, Kathryn Whitenton and Jakob Nielsen, *How People Read on the Web* (Freemont, CA: Nielsen Norman Group, 2015), p. 12.

3 Steve Krug, *Don't Make Me Think, Revisited: A Common Sense Approach to Web Usability* (San Francisco: New Riders, 2014), pp. 34–5.

4 Siegfried Vögele, *Handbook of Direct Mail: The Dialogue Method of Direct Written Sales Communication* (New York: Prentice Hall, 1992; first published 1984), pp. 186–202.

5 George Lucas, *Screenwriting for Anyone: How You Can Write Your Own Screenplay in 30 Days* (North Charleston: CreateSpace, 2015), pp. 8–9.

6 Yellowlees Douglas, *The Reader's Brain: How Neuroscience Can Make You a Better Writer* (Cambridge: Cambridge University Press, 2015), p. 25.

7 Ibid., p. 25.

8 Deidre Barrett, 'Supernormal Stimuli', https://www.youtube.com/watch?v=Y3ObUIf9pcs.

9 Ibid.

10 Alex Smith, '"I Wish My Son Had Cancer": How Shock Tactics Raised My Charity's Profile', *Guardian*, 11 August 2014, http://www.theguardian.com/voluntary-sector-network/2014/aug/11/wish-my-son-had-cancer-shock-tactics-charity-advertising-campaign.

11 John Yorke, *Into the Woods: How Stories Work and Why We Tell Them* (London: Penguin, 2013), p. 122.

12 Susan M. Weinschenk, *100 Things Every Designer Needs to Know About People* (Berkeley: New Riders, 2011), p. 108.

13 Beryl McAlhone and David Stuart, *A Smile in the Mind* (London: Phaidon, 1996).

14 *The Copy Book: How Some of the Best Advertising Writers in the World Write Their Advertising* (London: Taschen, 2011), pp. 10–11.

15 Arne Dietrich, 'The Cognitive Neuroscience of Creativity', *Psychonomic Bulletin and Review* 11(6), p. 6.

16 Ibid., p. 10.

17 Weinschenk, *100 Things Every Designer Needs to Know*, p. 33.

18 Douglas, *The Reader's Brain*, p. 56.

6: How to Write Your Body Copy

1 *The Copy Book: How Some of the Best Advertising Writers in the World Write Their Advertising* (London: Taschen, 2011), p. 10.

2 Stephen King, *On Writing: A Memoir of the Craft* (London: Hodder, 2012; first published New York, 2000), p. 249.

3 *The Copy Book*, p. 110.

4 Doug Zanger, 'The Ever-Evolving Craft of Copy', *Advertising Week Social Club*, 28 August 2015, http://www.theawsc. com/2015/08/28/the-ever-evolving-craft-of-copy/.

5 *A Plain English Handbook: How to Create Clear SEC Disclosure Documents* (Washington, 1998), https://www.sec.gov/pdf/ handbook.pdf, p. 2.

6 Peter Vierod, 'How To Persuade Your People to Shed Their Writing Inhibitions', *The Friendly Persuader*, July 2015.

7 Siegfried Vögele, *Handbook of Direct Mail: The Dialogue Method of Direct Written Sales Communication* (New York: Prentice Hall, 1992; first published 1984), p. 266.

8 Hannah Furness, 'Joanna Trollope: You Cannot Be Great Novelist Until After 35', *Daily Telegraph*, 9 March 2015, http://www. telegraph.co.uk/news/celebritynews/11457677/Joanna- Trollope-You-cannot-be-great-novelist-until-after-35.html.

9 Tony Brignull, 'The Best of Us: Tony Brignull Pays Personal Tribute to David Abbott', *The Drum*, 6 August 2014, http:// www.thedrum.com/news/2014/08/06/best-us-tony-brignull- pays-personal-tribute-david-abbott.

10 Rory Sutherland, *The Wiki Man* (London: It's Nice That and Ogilvy Group UK, 2011), p. 156.

11 Vögele, *Handbook of Direct Mail*, p. 55.

12 *New Scientist*, 'Why Things Fall Apart', 15 August 2015.

13 Susan M. Weinschenk, *100 Things Every Designer Needs to Know About People* (Berkeley: New Riders, 2011), p. 218.

14 Anita Charlesworth, 'Nudge, Nudge! How the Sugar Tax Will Help British Diets', *Financial Times*, 19/20 March, 2016.

15 Sutherland, *The Wiki Man*, p. 31.

7: Your Second Draft: Put These Things In

1 '(Not) the End: London's stage people don't hesitate to rewrite plays', *Philadelphia Inquirer*, 14 August 1989.

2 Steve Krug, *Don't Make Me Think, Revisited: A Common Sense Approach to Web Usability* (San Francisco: New Riders, 2014), p. 39.

3 Stephen King, *On Writing: A Memoir of the Craft* (London: Hodder, 2012; first published New York, 2000), p. 130.

4 Robert Lacey and Danny Danziger, *The Year 1000: What Life Was Like At The Turn Of The First Millennium* (London: Little, Brown, 1999), p. 30.

5 Haruki Murakami, 'The Moment I Knew I Would Be a Novelist', *Daily Telegraph*, 25 July 2015, http://www.telegraph.co.uk/ books/authors/haruki-murakami-the-moment-I-knew-I-would-be-a-novelist/.

6 *The Copy Book: How Some of the Best Advertising Writers in the World Write Their Advertising* (London: Taschen, 2011), p. 10.

7 Ian Harris, 'Three Ways to Write Like Warren Buffett', *Management Today*, 27 February 2015, http://www. managementtoday.co.uk/news/1334430/three-ways-write-warren-buffett/.

8 Stephen King, *On Writing*, p. 137.

9 Susan Greenfield, 'On Storytelling', https://vimeo. com/33716283.

10 Yellowlees Douglas, *The Reader's Brain: How Neuroscience Can Make You a Better Writer* (Cambridge: Cambridge University Press, 2015), p. 57.

11 Dominik Imseng, *Ugly Is Only Skin-Deep: The Story of the Ads that Changed the World* (Kibworth, Leicester: Matador, 2016), p. 58.

12 Stephen King, *On Writing*, pp. 138–9.

13 Steve Krug, *Don't Make Me Think, Revisited*, p. 50.

14 Tony Brignull, 'The Eternal Appeal of Abraham Lincoln's Gettysburg Address, by Tony Brignull, D&AD's Most Awarded Copywriter', *The Drum*, 20 November 2013, http://www.thedrum.com/opinion/2013/11/20/eternal-appeal-abraham-lincolns-gettysburg-address-tony-brignull-dads-most.

15 Rudolf Flesch, *How to Write Plain English: A Book for Lawyers and Consumers* (New York: Barnes & Noble, 1981). See http://pages.stern.nyu.edu/~wstarbuc/Writing/Flesch.htm

16 Ibid.

17 Jakob Nielsen and John Morkes, 'Concise, SCANNABLE, and Objective: How to Write for the Web', 1 January 1997, https://www.nngroup.com/articles/concise-scannable-and-objective-how-to-write-for-the-web/

18 Greenfield, 'On Storytelling'.

8: Your Third Draft: Cut These Things Out

1 Alex Singleton, *The PR Masterclass: How to Develop a Public Relations Strategy That Works* (Chichester: Wiley, 2014), pp. 80–1.

2 Daniel Kahneman, *Thinking, Fast and Slow* (London: Penguin, 2012; first published New York, 2012), p. 63.

3 *Why Your Copywriter Looks Sad* (London: DMA, 2015).

4 *The Copy Book: How Some of the Best Advertising Writers in the World Write Their Advertising* (London: Taschen, 2011), p. 10.

10: How to Lay Your Copy Out

1 Jakob Nielsen, 'Legibility, Readability, and Comprehension: Making Users Read Your Words', 15 November 2015, https://www.nngroup.com/articles/legibility-readability-comprehension/.

2 Colin Wheildon, *Type and Layout: Are You Communicating Or Are You Just Making Pretty Shapes?* (Mentone, Victoria: Worsley Press, 2005), pp. 45–8.

3 Sofie Beier, *Reading Letters: Designing for Legibility* (Amsterdam: Bis Publishers, 2012), p. 124.

4 Ibid., p. 125.

5 Ibid., p. 121.

6 Wheildon, *Type and Layout*, p. 53.

7 Ibid., pp. 48–53.

8 Kara Pernice, Kathryn Whitenton and Jakob Nielsen, *How People Read on the Web* (Freemont, CA: Nielsen Norman Group, 2015), p. 180.

9 Ibid., p. 12.

10 Wheildon, *Type and Layout*, p. 99.

11 Mary C. Dyson, 'How Physical Text Layout Affects Reading From Screen', *Behavioural Information Technology*, 123:6 (November–December, 2004), p. 391.

12 Ibid., p. 383.

13 Wheildon, *Type and Layout*, pp. 57–9.

14 Ibid., p. 99.

P.S. That was the theory. But what about the practice?

1 Mark Forsyth, *The Elements of Eloquence: How to Turn the Perfect English Phrase* (London: Icon Books, 2014), p. 1.

2 *Email Statistics Report, 2015–2019* (Palo Alto: Radicati Group Inc., 2015), p. 2.

3 Ibid., p. 4.

4 Peter C. Brown, Henry L. Roederer and Mark A. McDaniel, *Make It Stick: The Science of Successful Learning* (Cambridge, MA: Harvard University Press, 2014), p. 48.

Acknowledgements

On page 148, I say how important it is to show your writing to someone who 'is smart enough to see the flaws in your work, and confident enough to point them out to you.' Taking my own advice, I sent my manuscript to the following people; and now I'd like to thank them for the help they gave me.

Martin Bihl is the best reviewer of advertising books in the world. He did it for *Advertising Age* before starting The Agency Review where you'll find dozens of reviews, many of which are better written than the books themselves. When I asked Martin to look at my manuscript I said, 'I'd rather have a stinker from you now than when it's in print in six months' time.' He held his nose and went to work.

During my twenty years in agency life, Nigel Webb was one of the very few writers whose copy I never had to amend. Alas, I made a much bigger call on his time when the roles were reversed last November.

Tim Connor is an account director who writes the kind of briefs that the copywriters on page 29 are craving. He's even better at telling stories with words and music. Just as au fait with Bernstein as he is Bernbach, it was Tim who gave me the Sondheim quote on page 106 and, more importantly, put me on to, first, Siegfried Vögule's research into copywriting, and then John Yorke's treatise on storytelling. Bravo.

Tom Callaghan is a brilliant copywriter turned bestselling author of the bloodiest of thrillers. As I expected, when he handed back my manuscript, several pages were splattered with the colour red.

I cleaned up what I could and then, thankfully, in came the forensics experts: Olivia Morris (Editor) and Claire Gatzen (Desk Editor) at Pan Macmillan. Little if anything escaped their educated eyes.

Then there is John Gordon, who suggested I write the book, and Frances Wilson, who helped steer it through publication.

And finally, one other person deserves a mention. I tried to write this book in reportage style. My aim was to take you with me from the hard slog of the initial draft to the relief of reaching the first re-write, and the ups and downs of the edits and amends. I also wanted to share with you some ideas, headlines and copy I came across along the way. Starting in July 2015, I sent in my first draft on 8 February 2016. I then made amends and updates as layouts and proofs came back from the ever-attentive Claire Gatzen.

Throughout that time, my fiancée, Morag Brennan, saw little more of me than the back of my head and shoulders at the kitchen table. Except, that is, when I'd call her over and ask, 'Does this make sense?', 'Which of these paragraphs do you prefer?' and 'What do you want for breakfast?' (see page 63). I'm so very grateful for her patience, advice and good humour. I'm a lucky chap.

Index